Sisterly Feelings

Alan Ayckbourn

Sisterly Feelings

edited by
Gerard Gould

with a personal essay by
Alan Ayckbourn

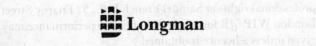
Longman

Longman Group UK Limited,
Longman House, Burnt Mill, Harlow,
Essex CM20 2JE, England
and Associated Companies throughout the world.

Copyright © Haydonning Ltd 1981
Published by arrangement with Chatto & Windus Ltd.,
London
This edition © Longman Group UK Limited 1989
Personal essay © Haydonning Ltd 1989

First published 1989

ISBN 0 582 01639 8

Set in 10/12 point Baskerville, Linotron 202
Produced by Longman Group (FE) Ltd
Printed in Hong Kong

Contents

Contents

A personal essay

by Alan Ayckbourn

Writing about sisters . . .

In 1974, Peter Hall invited me to write a play for the nearly completed National Theatre on London's South Bank. I visited the building during the final stages of its completion. It seemed vast. The two main auditoria, the Olivier and the Lyttelton, were empty shells without seats or stage walls. The tiny, temporary theatre-in-the-round which I was running in Scarborough (and where I initiate all my plays) would have fitted comfortably into either of them, twenty or thirty times.

I felt a little daunted. Peter suggested the Lyttelton, the proscenium stage, as being the more suitable of the two for my purposes (the National's very much smaller studio space, the Cottesloe, was still a hole in the ground with no fixed completion date). For my part, I determined that I should not break with tradition but adopt the same procedure for the National as I had been following in the past with the commercial theatre: that is première anything I wrote at the Scarborough theatre first. The result was *Bedroom Farce*, which Peter and I co-directed and which became one of the first really big new play successes that the NT had in their new building.

Inevitably, there had to be a sequel. This time, it was felt I should tackle the biggest of the theatres, the Olivier. This thousand-seat auditorium, with a semi-thrust stage, really did present a challenge, especially to someone used to writing (mainly for economic reasons) for casts of six to eight in tiny spaces. I had solved the size problem at the Lyttelton by writing a play set in three rooms side by side, thus effectively dividing the stage into three. The Olivier wasn't going to be so simple.

Again, I decided to launch the play in Scarborough and

once more I was to work at the National with a co-director, on this occasion the experienced and very supportive Christopher Morahan, who had earlier directed the television version of the NT's *Bedroom Farce*.

As I considered ideas, I came to the conclusion that in order to utilize the space most effectively, I should write something set outdoors. I have always welcomed the chance to write an exterior play and had already done several with garden settings (*Relatively Speaking, Time and Time Again*, one of *The Norman Conquests* and *Joking Apart*). But, on this occasion, I needed a setting that was potentially bigger than anything I had ever demanded before. The garden of a stately home? Or possibly a public space, say a public common?

So I set about writing *Sisterly Feelings* for the winter season of the 1978 Scarborough season. We had moved from our original home and the birth place of *Bedroom Farce*, Scarborough's Library Theatre, to a slightly larger (only *slightly* larger), more flexible auditorium in the Old Grammar School at Westwood, where we are today. Here, it was possible to alter the normal four-sided auditorium into a near three-sided one. By removing most of the seats from one block (but still leaving a few), we were able to 'create' a giant grass bank, going up twelve feet or so.

The play, you may gather, started life very much influenced by its physical requirements. But then I have always been firmly of the belief that a play is rarely just a single notion – rather it is, in essence, a meeting of several ideas. Put a few of them together and, like rabbits, they will start to breed if you're lucky. And though, of course, one of these ideas must be the theme of the play, theatre is – and this often seems forgotten – a visual as well as a verbal medium. Characters should not only discuss what they've done or what they're about to do (in fact, the less they do the better) but should also be *seen* to do it.

It all forms part of my *aren't-we-in-the-wrong-room?* theory. Simply, the acid test of a good play is whether the dramatist has put us, the audience, where we can expect the best view of the parade. The more he makes us feel, 'I'm sorry I missed that bit, I wish I'd been there instead of here', the more we experience an overwhelming curiosity as to what's going on backstage, the less well constructed his play is. Playwriting, at its most basic, is the business of arranging for the right people to be in the right place at the right time – without – and this is the difficult part – an audience being aware of it.

Whilst contemplating a suitable setting for the new play, I was also considering how, as a writer, I could make best use of the National Theatre itself – a company with larger resources and greater flexibility than the West End could offer. How to construct a play to take advantage of this flexibility? I started to consider an idea I'd been nursing for some time, the possibility of a play with limited 'random' action.

Clearly, the only real difference between theatre and, say, TV or film is that it's live. Every performance is unique and, certainly in the best theatre, is subject to a million different variations, depending upon the mood of the performer, the audience and the rapport that is established between them. And anyone who thinks that audiences don't vary has never taken part in a run of more than one consecutive performance!

Yet another ingredient was the fact that I'd wanted for some time to write about two sisters. The affection, the jealousy, the love–hate – but ultimately the love – that might exist between them. A story of how they would fight over the same, apparently ideal man. How his personality would alter subtly in response to each of them; how they themselves would alter with him. And how, in the end, ideal men – ideal anybodies, come to that – belong only in our dreams. Tall, bronzed, athletic Simon would appear at first to Abigail and Dorcas like a hero from a comic book. But in the end, it would be Patrick to whom Abigail would return, in need of his strength and humour; it would be impossible Stafford to whom Dorcas would, irresistibly, for better or worse, return as nursemaid.

Dorcas needed a relationship where she was at least an equal partner. Ultimately, she could never submit to Simon's appalling brand of paternalistic chauvinism. For Abigail, Simon's attempts to put her on a pedestal, although worship may be fine for goddesses, was going to prove equally unsatisfying.

Having sorted out the principal protagonists, it was then a matter of deciding how and when the play would vary. Obviously, if audiences were going to see the piece twice (and I hoped they would) I needed to make the scenes that were common to both versions – the ones that people would need to sit through more than once – as short as possible. There was no way I could vary the first scene at all. I had to make it as short as I could, just enough to introduce ten characters and set up the basic premise. At the end of it comes the first choice which I made as random as possible by employing the toss of a coin. Such a random decision not only had to be made, but, more important, it had to be *seen* to be made.

This led naturally to the twin cores of the play and progressed, at the end of the first act, to another possible shift of affections.

I decided to keep the first act variations within sight of each other. There are a lot of overlapping events – the same picnic (I'd always wanted to write a picnic scene), some identical dialogue, even the same wasp! This, as you might imagine, went down better with audiences than it did with actors who had a nightly dread of going into the wrong variation or, worse still, the wrong set of sandwiches!

In Act 2, events really diverge. Simon, our hero – or anti-hero, depending on how you see him – is beginning to show his real colours. Abigail, I felt, should have the night scene. I bought a small tent and set it up in my living room whilst I worked out the action at the camp site. For Dorcas, I chose to make full use of the hill. A cross country race seemed like fun and, given the competitive nature of Simon, would serve the dual purpose of further highlighting the choice Dorcas is faced with between him and Stafford. The only problem was how to get rid of the other 90 per cent of the cross country competitors.

The last scene is, like the first, always the same but it is possible, by change of emphasis and attitude – especially on the part of the protagonists Abigail, Dorcas, Stafford, Patrick and Simon – to play it in at least four different ways.

The main structure having been formed, it was then a matter of my weaving in the various related counter themes. Apart from the central five, Uncle Len, of course, plays a central role in both Abigail's and Dorcas's infidelities. Auntie Rita, apart from being pivotal in the picnic scenes, adds general family colour whilst Ralph gives the whole family a focal point around which to revolve.

And Brenda and Mel? Well, I needed amongst all the chopping and changings of our main characters, to have one constant private steady relationship. Something that says 'we're not *all* like this, some of us just get on with life quietly'. Both sisters are overprotective towards their younger brother; both are critical of Brenda and underestimate her entirely – typical, really, of older sisters. But in the end, Brenda and Melvyn have the last laugh, whereas Abigail and Dorcas are left a little sadder and wiser and resigned, for a time at least, to settle for what they already have. Maybe, after all, as in most of our relationships, we get what we deserve.

Introduction

Britain's most successful playwright

By the end of 1987 Alan Ayckbourn, at the age of forty-eight, had written thirty-four plays. Shakespeare's known total output amounts to thirty-eight plays. There is not a single week when some Ayckbourn is not being performed in a theatre somewhere in the British Isles. In 1987 three Ayckbourn plays could be seen in London theatres at the same time; in addition, he was responsible for three highly successful productions in the National Theatre. His plays have been translated into twenty-four languages. They are all comedies, although his more recent work reveals serious undertones.

Alan Ayckbourn was born in 1939 in Hampstead, a residential suburb in north London and much favoured by artists. His father was the leader of the London Symphony Orchestra; his mother a short-story writer for popular magazines. Most of his school life was spent in boarding schools including Haileybury, one of the major public schools with a long tradition of educating the sons of army officers. There was nothing in his own solidly middle-class upbringing to indicate that, one day, he would specialize in depicting the hopes and frustrations, longings and disillusions of very ordinary, lower middle-class characters.

As happens so frequently in British education, the enthusiasm of a stage-struck teacher exerted a great influence on an impressionable pupil. Ayckbourn's talent for writing and acting was discovered and fostered. Through this teacher he was introduced to Donald Wolfit, an actor-manager, famous for touring the country with his own Shakespeare productions. At the age of seventeen Alan Ayckbourn started as an assistant stage manager and learned the craft of theatre in the best possible, most practical way. In these days of strict Equity (the actors' union) regulations about employment in the theatre such tough training on the job is no longer possible.

In this way the young Alan Ayckbourn learned stage management, acting and directing through first-hand experience. When he became dissatisfied with the narrow range of acting parts that were given him, he began to write his own plays. Since then nearly every year has seen a new Ayckbourn play, sometimes more than one. *Sisterly Feelings* appeared in 1979. It gives a particularly appropriate recipe for an Ayckbourn success.

Take a family of lower-middle to middle-class social status in a suburban area within a radius of thirty to forty miles of London, show them in a moment of their lives when they might be expected to be most united but also most vulnerable (in this case, just after the funeral of their mother), introduce one or two characters outside the family unit (Simon and Stafford) who are then expected to disrupt the apparent harmony. Develop the story by presenting other family rituals (a picnic) which inevitably end in disaster. Focus on individual members (the two sisters), set them in conflict with one another through one of the outsiders but show them united in possessiveness when it comes to protecting a member of the tribe (Melvyn against Brenda). Finally, leave the family in an uneasy truce, seemingly united (a wedding) but with the certainty that future family occasions, however trivial the circumstances, will cause dangerous passions to erupt.

Audiences easily recognize these characters and situations. We do not necessarily identify them with ourselves, but these people, with all their insecurities, irritations and obsessions, are only too familiar. In the warm, communal atmosphere of the theatre we can afford to share in the fortunes and misfortunes of others without feeling in any way threatened. We can laugh at disasters which, if they happened to us, might not be quite so funny. An Ayckbourn play needs a live audience who will make an immediate response to the action on the stage. That is why the author prefers the theatre to radio, film and television. On some nights when the theatre is packed, the actors are on particularly good form and the audiences at their most responsive, the theatrical magic works to perfection.

A trip to Scarborough

Britain's most successful playwright lives in Scarborough, 250 miles from London. With a population of 43,000, Scarborough is the largest seaside resort in North Yorkshire. A trip to Scarborough to see the latest Ayckbourn play has now become an annual event for national and international critics.

At first sight Scarborough conveys a solidity which is traditionally associated with late-Victorian Britain: large, comfortable hotels overlooking the sweeping bays and serving rich, five-course Yorkshire dinners between six and seven o'clock to allow their clients to enjoy the evening entertainment; piers at either end of the town offering a variety of amusements for all ages; seaside promenades and cliff walks; well-cultivated gardens; solidly built stone houses with sash windows; good taste and respectability. Scarborough is a long way from the suburban sameness which breeds such boredom, frustrations and social conformity in Ayckbourn characters. The bracing air in all seasons of the year makes for a rugged individuality up north.

It was in Scarborough in 1955 that a theatrical revolution took place. In a space in the local public library Stephen Joseph, a director, pioneered theatre in the round. Audiences were seated on four sides surrounding a performing area in the middle. The actors made their entrances and exits through the four corridors between the seats. In this way good use was made of a limited space; a much greater intimacy between the actor and the audience was created; simplicity and truthfulness became the keynotes of a production. The actors were much more exposed; they could not get away with conventional acting techniques.

It was this company which the young Alan Ayckbourn joined in 1957. At first they played only a summer season of twelve weeks in Scarborough and toured the Midlands for the rest of the year. Now the theatre is open throughout the whole year. From 1959 onwards Alan Ayckbourn wrote a play for every summer season. The seventh play (*Relatively Speaking*) became a great success, was transferred to a London theatre with a starry cast and is still being revived. After Stephen Joseph's untimely death Alan Ayckbourn became the artistic director of the company. The pattern was set for a new play to open in Scarborough, a transfer to London with well-known actors after the Scarborough season, a long run in London's West End and later a tour of provincial theatres.

To cope with the success, a new venue was made available in Scarborough. Aptly named after its founder, the Stephen Joseph Theatre-in-the-Round is now housed in a Further Education college. Situated in a little side street near the town centre, it has one main auditorium with raked seats and a studio for lunchtime and late night shows with tables for buffet meals. Not every production is in the round; sometimes the audience is seated on three sides. The theatre is popular with both the permanent inhabitants and the visitors. The town is proud of its famous resident dramatist.

In his turn, Alan Ayckbourn is appreciative of Scarborough's amenities, not least of its annual cricket festival. Away from the pressures of London, apart from a two-year stint at the National Theatre, this shrewd observer of the English social scene lives in a typically English seaside town and can indulge in the most English of all hobbies: playing and watching cricket. No wonder that his view of theatre has never lost its sense of fun.

Fun and games

Television has accustomed us to the treatment of social issues and problems through drama. Sometimes these are presented in a serious, documentary way. At other times they are the subjects of absurd situation comedies with exaggerated characters playing to a predictable laughter response from an invited audience. It is Alan Ayckbourn's great achievement as a writer that, despite such an enormous output to his credit, he has never lost his sense of fun. Nor have his characters lost their credibility. The theatre is a place to him where nothing is impossible. Here are some examples to show how he has extended the normal limitation of a stage to offer only one setting at any one time:

How the Other Half Loves – two sitting-rooms superimposed on one another;

The Norman Conquests – three plays dealing with the same theme and people but seen from three different areas of the same house (dining-room, sitting-room, garden);

Bedroom Farce – three bedrooms on permanent view;

Way Upstream – a cabin cruiser moving on a river;

A Small Family Business – the inside of an entire modern house (including staircase, corridors, bathroom, toilet) which is also interchangeable with the interior of similar houses inhabited by other characters.

Ayckbourn's skill is not just confined to inventing unusual settings. These become the springboard from which to launch a series of high-spirited attacks on all too human failings and obsessions. Look at the following scene from *Just Between Ourselves* (from *Joking Apart*, Penguin, 1976). The setting is a garage of a 'medium-price executive house on a private estate'. Dennis, the owner, prides himself on being a bit of a do-it-yourself man. See how he is trying to sell his wife's car to Neil.

DENNIS   You've come about the car, haven't you?

NEIL   That's right.

DENNIS   Well, there she is. Have a look for yourself. That's the one.

NEIL   Ah.

DENNIS   Now, I'll tell you a little about it, shall I? Bit of history. Number one, it's not my car. It's the wife's. However, now before you say – ah ah, woman driver – she's been very careful with it. Never had a single accident in it, touch wood. Well I mean, look, you can see hardly a scratch on it. Considering the age. To be perfectly honest, just between ourselves, she's a better driver than me – when she puts her mind to it. I mean, look – considering it's, what now – seven – nearly eight years old. Just look for yourself at that bodywork.

NEIL Yes, yes.

DENNIS I bought it four years ago for her. It was then as good as new – virtually. Three years old and as good as new it was.

NEIL It looks very good.

DENNIS It is really, amazingly good.

NEIL I suppose being under cover . . .

DENNIS Ah yes, well, quite. As I was just about to say, being under cover as it is.

NEIL Important.

DENNIS Vital. Vital to keep a car under cover. I mean, frankly that's why we want to get rid of it. I want to get my own car under cover. I don't know if you saw it when you were coming in, parked just out there, on the road there.

NEIL Yes, I think I . . .

DENNIS It's doing it no good at all. It's an urgent priority to get that car under cover. You've got a garage, I take it?

NEIL No.

DENNIS Ah. Well, when I say that, with a car like this one, it's not as vital as with some cars. I mean, this one, (*he slaps the bonnet*) this is a very, very sturdy vehicle indeed. As a matter of fact, they're not even making them any more. Not this particular model. They took up too much raw material. They're not economic to make. There's a lot of raw material in this. Mind you, there's no problem with parts. They're still making the parts, they're just not making the cars. Not that you'll ever need a part. We've never needed a part not in four years. No, as a matter of fact, I'll let you into a little secret. This car has barely been out of this garage in six months.

NEIL   Really?

DENNIS   Barely been out. As a matter of fact, frankly, just between ourselves, the wife's had a few, what shall I say, health worries and she hasn't really been up to driving.

NEIL   Oh, I'm sorry to . . .

DENNIS   Oh, she's better now. She's very much better now. But she's gone off driving altogether. You can see, look – look at that clock there – I'll be surprised if it's done fifty thousand. Here we are. Fifty-five thousand two hundred and fifty-two miles . . . well, fifty-five, fifty thousand, round about that figure.

NEIL   Amazing.

DENNIS   Peanuts for a car like this. It's hardly run in.

You can imagine how the scene develops. The garage door is jammed; the car fails to start. But Dennis remains hearty and jovial, covering up any human feeling with a blustering laugh. Words have lost any meaning with him. We all know people like Dennis, blundering through life without any regard for other people's feelings. This scene is enormous fun for both actors and audiences, but the laughter becomes uneasy. Dennis goes on to destroy his wife's mental balance, the logical conclusion to a process which began when he talked about 'the wife' to a total stranger. It was Ayckbourn's aim to 'write a totally effortless, totally truthful, unforced comedy shaped like a flawless diamond in which one can see a million reflections, both one's own and other people's'.

Male chauvinism is a source of fun in *Sisterly Feelings*. Policeman Len, whose one day of glory is the annual cross-country race, finds it difficult to cope when most of his police helpers have been called away to guard a demon-

stration. This is how he talks to Dorcas after she has volun-
teered to stand at a checkpoint:

> LEN   It's a crying shame all this, you know. I mean, it takes
> months to organize these things. I don't know if you
> appreciate that. I mean, as a start-off, you've got your
> officials, your catering, your first-aid, your toilet facilities.
> You've got the course to mark. A thousand things to think
> of, you know.
>
> DORCAS   Yes, yes.
>
> LEN   And now look at it. I mean, pardon me but it's a
> tragic fact that we're that undermanned that I've had to
> resort to five women.

Len's instructions to Dorcas are then delivered as if he was
speaking to a small and not very bright child.

Simon, the sex object of both sisters, has his ego deflated in
both versions of the play. He suffers the humiliation of seeing
both women reject him and return to their former men.

Although Ayckbourn extracts every ounce of fun out of his
characters, he is never patronising or condescending to them.
Beneath the fun there is some cruelty. Abigail and Dorcas are
cruel to their future sister-in-law, but Brenda gets her own
back in the end. We laugh at all these people, but they are
quite resilient. When the laughter has died down, we ask
ourselves: 'Are we really like this?' And the answer surely is:
'*We* are not, but we know many people who are.'

Another great skill is the playwright's sheer inventiveness.
Ayckbourn is fascinated by the unending possibilities 'play'
offers him. After all, the word 'play' is the same when it refers
to children's amusement or to adults' dramatic entertainment.
Tossing a coin often starts a game. In *Sisterly Feelings* it decides
which particular version of the play is to be played. This is
a novel and bold technique to introduce in the theatre. It
involves a great deal of risk. For one thing, the actors have to
learn two versions of the play. These are sufficiently similar

in dialogue to lead to confusion. For another, the stage management must be prepared for whichever version is to be played as they require different properties for the actors to bring on and handle. The box office staff must be kept informed so that audiences buying tickets are not misled. In fact, the entire theatre and production staff are kept on their toes whenever this play is performed.

Playing games is part of the ritual that Ayckbourn enjoys to make a focal point in his drama. Not just the obvious ones like cricket (*Time and Time Again*, 1971) and a cross-country derby in this play but also, in a much more subtle way, the games that people play to deceive their partners in marriage. Abigail tries very hard to seduce Simon not only to score over her sister but also to make her husband jealous. She plays a dangerous game, but she wins.

The agonies of everyday life

Pendon, the fictitious place where the action of *Sisterly Feelings* is set, is sharply defined. It is an example of suburbia, an ever-growing residential area expanding beyond the Common. In the centre would be old Pendon with its High Street shops, banks, building society and house agents branches, supermarkets and shopping precincts. The 'new' Pendon would consist of a number of estates within which the houses would show a remarkable uniformity of shape and design, bungalows, semi-detached and detached.

'Upward mobility', the process by which first-time buyers of modest dwellings gradually improve their social status by acquiring larger and better properties in more desirable surroundings in the same district, would be a noticeable feature of Pendon. Pendon is in the south, and building societies, which lend money to potential house buyers, are making a good business.

Suburban existence can be pleasant, but it can also breed

a dangerous pattern of life. Where streets and houses can all look the same, where neighbours can easily observe one another, certain activities like washing the car on Saturday afternoon or Sunday morning become a regular ritual. Boredom is a particular enemy. Any break in the daily routine may assume an importance beyond its proportion. Abigail, in Act 2, Scene 1 *Abigail*, gives voice to her pent-up feelings on this subject:

> I need this adventure, this excitement. I couldn't simply go on running your little castle. It was getting so boring. I know, we had wonderful times, occasionally, but we always met the same people. And we'd started getting into the same routines. We watched this programme on Monday and we went to the pub on Saturdays. I thought, God, I'll be old and I'll have done nothing. I'll be like all those other dreadful women with their shopping baskets on wheels having coffee in the back of the delicatessen. And I'm worth more than that. A bloody sight more than that. (pages 103–4)

Patrick, to whom this cry of inner pain is addressed, has his own world. Abigail, at twenty-six, is bored and has no resources with which to cope with the 'littleness of life'. And so the prospect of a horribly uncomfortable night under canvas with Simon becomes a big adventure.

Abigail gives more utterance to the agonies of everyday life than some of the other characters. About married life:

> . . . we don't discuss anything anyway. Unless it appears on Patrick's official breakfast time agenda. And that consists mainly of food. Minutes of the last meal and proposals for the next. (page 24)

Patrick believes you get out of life 'what you put into it'. Abigail's anguished reply is: 'I've flung the lot in and it's disappeared without trace.' She blames 'this awful civilizing domesticating streak' in women for curbing their 'natural selves' and 'to settle for the second-best.' Her frustrated feelings lead her to fling herself foolishly at Simon:

> I'm afraid I seem to have got the reputation as the one who chews men up for breakfast and then spits them out in small pieces. I think it's still considered rather unbecoming for women to have large appetites. (page 67–8)

She genuinely feels that she is being wasted.

Dorcas, the unmarried sister, still has hopes. Life with Stafford, the scruffy, chaotic, would-be poet sponger and political activist, may be maddening, but it is not boring. She wants to break out of her daily routine and also flings herself at Simon. When Stafford gives her proof of his attempts to become 'ordinary' and 'boring' by giving up politics, poetry, smoking and doing exercises and growing 'unnecessary muscles' to become more like Simon, Dorcas immediately rejects all this. She prefers the old, unreformed Stafford.

Boredom, frustrations, routines lead to minor squabbles and major quarrels. In such circumstances a misunderstanding about which sandwiches to bring to a picnic is blown up into a major crisis. Dorcas sums up such agonising: 'It happens every bloody time we have a picnic.'

Sneering at other people is another outcome of repressed feelings. Both sisters find Brenda too dreary for words. But it is Patrick, the male chauvinist, who is the chief culprit. His attack on Abigail is satire at its best, but it has a lethally serious aim:

> ... I know women's metabolisms go round and round in cycles but you're the only one I know who has cycles within cycles. Today is your day for not carrying things. Yesterday was your refusing-to-shut-any-doors day. Monday, if I'm not mistaken, was the yearly anniversary for the start of your leaving-all-the-taps-running week. I mean, I don't mind as

long as I know they're coming. But it is nice to mark these
celebrations, don't you agree? Otherwise we'll miss them.
Like the International Open Fridge Door Overnight Festival
or the All British Leaving the Oven on Low Week or the
Jubilee Celebration for . . . (pages 54–5)

Abigail angrily interrupts this flow of sarcasm. She is very
close to tears.

Right at the end of the play, both sisters make it only too
clear that they are likely to return to their original life style.
They depart from our sight with a renewed attack on their
sister-in-law Brenda: 'Mel's not getting stuck with that . . .'

Ayckbourn shows us human desperation breaking through
restrictive forms of life. We laugh, but we are always aware
of the pain beneath.

An actor's delight

(This is a discussion between the Editor and Nigel Cooke, an
actor who has not only appeared in several Ayckbourn plays
but who has also had the experience of being directed by the
playwright.)

EDITOR   Alan Ayckbourn always lives in the hope that 'one
   night somewhere, the chemistry will be right. The right
   cast will meet the right audience in the right theatre, and
   something rich and rewarding will be shared between
   them'. What do you think he means by that?

ACTOR   It is the ultimate goal in theatre to have actors and
   audience at one with each other so that the audience's
   anticipation and reaction become a part of the play itself.
   Both are giving and receiving in equal amounts.

EDITOR   How do you think this is achieved?

ACTOR   I wish there was an easy answer to that. There must
   be a million ingredients that go into making theatre work.

It's like having a party: you can organise everything perfectly with lots of good friends, food, drink, music. And yet the party might not get off the ground ... people weren't relaxed. Another night – with the same basic ingredients – for some unaccountable reason, everything takes off. You can't have really good theatre without good writing. One of the things that makes Ayckbourn such a good writer is that he's always aware of his audience. It's an extremely tall order to mould hundreds of different people into a whole, but it's the writer's and actor's task, and Ayckbourn revels in it.

EDITOR What else do you think makes him the playwright he is?

ACTOR His characters are always identifiable and, there-fore, accessible. Above all, they are real. I believe that, in varying degrees, there's something of himself in all his characters, male and female. He never allows his audience to retreat and say 'that simply wouldn't happen'. For instance, at the end of the second act of *Time and Time Again*, when Leonard, the chief character, is busy seducing his best friend's fiancée, in his brother-in-law's garden pond, dressed in ill-fitting cricket wear, the audience completely gives into it, because all the stepping stones leading up to this moment have been skilfully laid. There is a crafted logic to his writing that is perfect and that demands a perfection of playing at all times.

EDITOR Please explain.

ACTOR You have to match his ear for language and rhythm. In them lie many character clues, and you have to match them as accurately as possible. You change Ayckbourn's words at your peril. A 'but' instead of an 'and' could break the logic. You must always honour his intentions. He writes *seriously* funny plays. In performance it is easy to be seduced by the audience's appreciation of the funny parts to the exclusion of everything else. You must not go over the top.

EDITOR What do you mean by that?

ACTOR Overdoing an effect. If there is a legitimate laugh to be had by slamming a door, don't do it twice. The play loses its momentum, the logic is broken again, and the audience starts to watch actors for their door-slamming ability, which isn't Ayckbourn's intention.

EDITOR What is his overall intention, do you think?

ACTOR He likes to show us what ridiculously horrible messes we make of our own and other people's lives. He likes to take a group of ordinary, ill-matched people and push them into extreme situations in which almost anything could happen but always within the realms of credibility.

EDITOR As an illustration, in *Sisterly Feelings* we can all recognise the Abigails of this world – the married woman bored with her husband, but not many Abigails would experience the events of that night under canvas. And yet there's not one moment in that scene that strikes one as being unreal.

ACTOR Exactly. And it is in such scenes, particularly, when we have our 'ups and downs' with our fellow actors, that perfection of playing is demanded from us.

EDITOR What makes Ayckbourn so remarkable as a director, not only of his own but also of other people's plays?

ACTOR More important than anything, he likes actors. He is always hungry for what an actor can bring to a part. He gives you free rein, space in which to breathe and expand, and actors invariably respond well to that. He is very protective of his actors. I found that, if I had a difficulty about a particular scene, he would take the pressure off me by focusing on another character's function within the same scene. This would allow me the opportunity to look at things objectively and begin to see my character's position in a completely fresh way. In an odd way, you don't know how you've been directed, but you have. You have to listen to him all the time. He can talk endlessly around the characters in relation to each other. He frequently speculates on what would have happened if so and so hadn't decided to visit so and so. Within a few minutes he's talked you through a whole new play, all the time slipping in details which are priceless in terms of value to the actor.

EDITOR So how does he rehearse?

ACTOR Hard, with tons of energy (mental and physical) and a lot of fun. He doesn't do warm-ups; he doesn't improvise. He likes actors to have learnt their lines as soon as possible. He will very quickly establish a basic structure of moves. These can be changed in rehearsal, but, more often than not, you realise his initial idea was the right one. He's a great technician and doesn't mind rehearsing his actors technically. As I've said, there are long chats. He has to stop himself sometimes, because, however fascinating and informative they are, he knows there's no substitute for the actor getting on and doing it for him or herself.

EDITOR Are you more aware of Ayckbourn the director or the author?

ACTOR They are one. When we ask questions, it is only to gain a better understanding of the text, never to change it. We are secure in that and in the knowledge that he's watching with a hawkeye that we're hitting the right notes at the right time.

EDITOR Does this double rôle make for any tensions?

ACTOR Certainly none that he wilfully imposes. The only tension I felt was of wanting to do my best for him. A healthy tension, I think.

EDITOR What is it like to play in the round as you do in Scarborough?

ACTOR Thrilling. It's how he conceives his plays. The audience can see everything. The actor can hide nowhere. The reaction becomes as important as the action – the audience as important as the actors. It makes for immediate and intimate playing; the audience's response is immediate. When you're in the middle of a hilariously funny scene and suddenly a character treats someone in a way which is definitely 'below the belt', you can hear the audience drawing in their breath not knowing what they've witnessed is funny, savage or what, then you know you're hitting the right notes. This is part of the chemistry I think Ayckbourn strives for.

Ayckbourn is a serious man of the theatre whose perception of what will work on a stage is extremely shrewd. In another way I see him as a small boy who sits at the water's edge lobbing in the odd firework (heavily disguised as a pebble) and watches with equal intensity the initial ripples, the explosion and then the aftermath.

Before reading the play

These questions are designed for use as an introduction to the play. They are particularly suitable for group work. The aim is for the students to bring personal experience to some of the themes which the play illustrates. The reading of the text will then become more meaningful and rewarding. Groups may be encouraged to make notes during discussion and then to report, using the notes, a summary to the whole class.

Families

Think of some recent family occasions in which you took part: birthdays, weddings, funerals, picnics, Christmas celebrations. What do you remember about these events? Describe one such occasion to the other members of your group. Was there anything special about it? Which members of the family made the strongest impression on you that day? For what reasons? Try to remember not just the people who were present but also the setting. Was it indoors or outdoors? What do you feel about such family gatherings? Do you look forward to them or do you dread them?

Choices

In *Sisterly Feelings* both actors and audiences are offered four combinations of different versions of the same play. They are faced with a choice. What does it mean having to make a choice? When did you personally have to make a choice? How did you make it? Was it the right or wrong choice at that time? Would you make the same choice now?

Discuss the following problem. A child has been given a small amount of money to buy sweets. He or she can buy either a larger quantity of the cheapest or a smaller amount of a better selection. What advice would you give the child?

Are we always free to make choices?

Sisterly Feelings

Sisterly Feelings

First presented at the Stephen Joseph Theatre-in-the-Round, Scarborough. Subsequently presented at the Olivier Theatre, National Theatre, London on the 3rd June 1980, with the following cast of characters:

DR RALPH MATTHEWS	Andrew Cruickshank
LEN COKER	Michael Bryant
RITA COKER	Susan Williamson
ABIGAIL SMYTHE	Penelope Wilton
PATRICK SMYTHE	Michael Gambon
DORCAS MATTHEWS	Anna Carteret
MELVYN MATTHEWS	Greg Hicks
BRENDA GRIMSHAW	Selina Cadell
SIMON GRIMSHAW	Stephen Moore
STAFFORD WILKINS	Simon Callow
MURPHY	Michael Fenner
MAJOR LIDGETT	Gordon Whiting

The play directed by Alan Ayckbourn and Christopher Morahan

Setting by Alan Tagg

The action takes place in a remote corner of Pendon Common

ACT I	Scene 1	February, Thursday afternoon
	Scene 2	June, Sunday afternoon
ACT II	Scene 1	September, Saturday afternoon
	Scene 2	November, Saturday afternoon

Time – the present

Act One

Scene 1   Prologue

A remote corner of Pendon Common. About 2.30 p.m. on a cold, damp day in late February

A steep grassy bank with planked steps cut into it allows access to the top and, presumably, the view over the rest of the Common beyond. At the foot of this bank, a grassy area flat and lush like a meadow. There is the odd patch of bramble about, perhaps the occasional small tree. Three-quarters of the way up the bank, a plain one-plank bench set in a concrete plinth

An occasional bird is heard perhaps, maybe the distant rumble of traffic on the main Pendon to Reading road

Incongruously, the meadow area is occupied by ten figures all in black or dark clothes. Clearly a funeral party. First, Dr Ralph Matthews, a robust man of seventy. Next to him, his brother-in-law, Len Coker, Detective Inspector in the local force. A sallow fifty-year-old, awkward in his unaccustomed best dark suit. With Len, his wife Rita, a woman of forty-five with the air of one persecuted by fate. Next, the eldest of Ralph's three children, Abigail, aged twenty-six. Like her brother and sister, she has a somewhat naïve air and her impetuosity has only been slightly dulled by two years' marriage to Patrick Smythe, her husband aged thirty. Dorcas, Abigail's sister, twenty-four. There is at first glance a superficial resemblance between the two women. Dorcas stands with her current 'attachment', Stafford Wilkins, also aged about twenty-four. He is a thin, unkempt young man who gives the impression of having inner fires that have been dampened by ceaseless disappointment. He is dressed or perhaps he has been dressed to suit the occasion, but it is evidently from a limited wardrobe. The youngest of Ralph's children is Melvyn, twenty years old and although at present subdued by the recent funeral, still very much young, confident and greatly in love. The object of his affections, his fiancée, Brenda, nineteen years old, clings to his arm. A pleasant if rather dead-pan girl. Beside them, finally, standing

1

slightly apart as befits a comparative stranger to the group, Simon Grim-
shaw, Brenda's older brother – a good-looking, well-built man of twenty-
eight. He is distinguished further by an un-English tan. The group stand
now silent and respectful. Ralph has apparently said something recently
and has now paused reflectively. The others wait for him to continue

RALPH   (*eventually*) Yes . . .

RITA   (*agreeing*) Mmm. Mmm.

LEN   Fancy.

RALPH   That was twenty-eight years ago, mark you. I'm going
back a bit now.

RITA   Oh yes. You're going back twenty-eight years.

LEN   Nearly thirty years, yes.

RALPH   There used to be a bench, you see. You know what
I mean by a bench? A public bench? It was around here
somewhere. Gone now.

ABIGAIL   There's a bench over there, Father.

RITA   Oh yes, look, there's one over there.

RALPH   (*slightly irritable*) No, no, no. This was a different
bench. Totally different. It wasn't that one. That bench is
recent. That's only been here a matter of, what . . .?

LEN   They have to replace those benches every three or four
years, you know. I mean, once the vandals get at them
. . .

RALPH   Four or five years. Five years at the most.

LEN   I mean, it used to be three or four years but the way
things are going now it's probably nearer every year. These
days.

RITA   These days. Yes.

LEN   I mean, we in the Police Force, we do what we can but
there's nothing we can do, you see. We're powerless. I mean,
the time was you'd catch your vandal on the job, over your
knees and wallop. No hard feelings. But nowadays, legis-
lation favours the vandal . . .

RITA   The police are powerless. Len's powerless.

RALPH   (*who has not been listening*) Yes, yes . . .

LEN   Anyway, that's where your benches go, if you want to know.

PATRICK   Time's getting on, Ralph, if you want to . . .

RALPH   Yes. I just wanted to . . . I just wanted to show everybody something . . .

ABIGAIL   Does it have to be today, Pa?

RALPH   It's only at the top there. Just a few steps.

PATRICK   (*to himself*) Oh my God. (*He looks at his watch*)

RALPH   You remember this place, Dorcas? Abi? You remember us all coming out here?

DORCAS   Yes, Pa, for picnics.

RALPH   Picnics, yes. I think you were too young weren't you, Melvyn?

MELVYN   No, I remember.

RALPH   (*riding over this as he has a habit of doing, to Len and Rita*) He'd've been too young, you see. He was an afterthought, that boy. Amy and I'd forgotten all about it by the time we had him. Wonderful picnics we had, Len. Your sister and I.

Brenda snuggles up to Melvyn. Rita starts struggling up the slope, semi-assisted by Len

MELVYN   You cold?

BRENDA   No, I'm fine.

RALPH   No, follow on, everyone. I insist that you see this view. If you haven't seen it, it's really – well, it's a marvellous view right over the Common. Can you manage, Rita?

RITA   Yes. Yes, it's just this . . .

LEN   Here, lean on me properly. You'll be all right.

Ralph moves fairly nimbly up the slope. Melvyn, Brenda and Simon move forward to follow. Len struggles with Rita

DORCAS   (*watching this*) Oh dear. Why does he always choose days like this . . .

LEN   (*seeing Melvyn and Brenda are trying to get past*) Let the young ones through, Rita.

3

RITA Oh yes, let them get past.

MELVYN Thank you.

Ralph vanishes momentarily over the top of the hill. Melvyn and Brenda slip past the struggling Rita and follow Ralph. Simon lingers, wondering whether to help

ABIGAIL (*to Patrick*) O.K.?

PATRICK Perfect.

SIMON (*tentatively to Len and Rita*) Could I . . .?

RITA (*offering a hand*) Oh, would you?

SIMON Certainly.

LEN Careful.

ABIGAIL Are you coming up?

PATRICK No. I think I'd prefer to stand here and watch the last of my fifty-guinea shoes sinking slowly into the mud.

LEN Careful, careful.

RITA Ooh.

SIMON (*who is being too hearty with her*) Sorry.

RITA It's my knee, you see.

ABIGAIL Well, why do you keep standing there, darling? Why don't you stand on firm ground?

PATRICK Because there is none, my sweet. There is no firm ground. We are standing in a marsh.

LEN Has it locked?

RITA I think it has.

SIMON I'm most awfully sorry.

PATRICK You see, we all somewhat foolishly came dressed for a funeral. We steeled ourselves to face perhaps some light breezes; maybe a little rain round the graveside; the odd bit of churchyard gravel underfoot. We came prepared for that. But your father, in his wisdom, has decided instead to lead us all into a bloody swamp.

Ralph reappears at the top

DORCAS Patrick . . .

4

RALPH What's your husband rabbiting about down there, Abi?

ABIGAIL Nothing.

Len and Simon lower Rita on to the bench

LEN Down you go, down you go.

RITA Yes, yes, that's it.

LEN I think you'll have to have another look at Rita's knee again, Ralph, if you would.

RALPH Nothing I can do for that knee – delightful though it is. She needs an operation. I've told her that.

RITA I'm not having an operation. I'd sooner have the knee.

PATRICK Ralph, could I briefly remind you that I had arranged to deliver you back home by two forty-five.

RALPH (*to Rita*) Then you'll have to put up with it, won't you? You know, Len, I think this was the bench.

RITA Next thing I know, they'll have my leg off.

PATRICK (*without conviction*) Two forty-five, Ralph, I do have a meeting . . . (*To himself*) As if that matters a damn to anyone.

ABIGAIL I'll remind him.

PATRICK Please do or I shall go without you.

ABIGAIL Patrick . . .!

PATRICK Five minutes. Then I'm off.

Patrick goes off to the car

ABIGAIL (*calling vainly after him*) We can't all get home in one car. Oh God.

DORCAS He won't go.

ABIGAIL Don't you believe it . . .

Abigail goes off after Patrick

LEN (*to Rita*) Right, are you fit?

RITA (*struggling to her feet*) Yes, yes.

RALPH (*returning to them*) Come and look at this view. It's absolutely stunning.

SIMON (*offering to help Len*) Can I . . .?

LEN No, no.

RITA No, no, no.

LEN Leave her to me.

Len and Rita slowly disappear over the brow of the hill

RALPH (*as they go*) You'd be better off with a wooden leg, anyway, Rita. Drop of linseed oil, that's all you'd ever need.

RITA Oh, don't say things like that.

Len and Rita exit

RALPH Dorcas, you coming up?

DORCAS No, we'll wait here, Pa, if you don't mind. We're not dressed for mountaineering. Besides we have seen it.

RALPH (*seeing Stafford*) What about thing? Young thing there.

Stafford, who is crouching studying blades of grass intently, does not hear

DORCAS Stafford?

STAFFORD Eh?

RALPH Come up here, boy, have a look at the view. You look as if you need the exercise.

DORCAS (*gently*) Go on.

STAFFORD (*reluctantly*) All right. (*He starts slowly up the slope, pulling out a cigarette as he does so*)

RALPH (*meanwhile*) You know, Dorcas, I think this was the bench you know. It's the very same one I proposed to your mother on. Isn't that extraordinary?

DORCAS Good heavens.

RALPH (*as Stafford draws close to him*) And don't light that. You don't need a cigarette. You want some air. You keep smoking those things, you'll get full of soot. (*Calling*) I'm telling him, Dorcas, if he keeps smoking these, you'll have to have him swept.

DORCAS Nothing to do with me.

STAFFORD (*disappearing over the hill*) Oh, Jesus . . .

Stafford goes

RALPH   We really must have a picnic again, you know. As soon as the weather's better. One Sunday. When you're home.

DORCAS   Lovely.

RALPH   Great fun. What's the matter with that boy?

DORCAS   How do you mean?

RALPH   He's always miserable. I've never seen him smile. Does he ever smile at you?

DORCAS   Sometimes.

RALPH   A woman needs to be smiled at, you know. Good for them. What is it? His stomach?

DORCAS   No. His principles.

RALPH   Oh God help him. No cure for those.

Abigail returns, holding Ralph's scarf

ABIGAIL   Pa, if you're going to gallivant around like this, for heaven's sake put your scarf on, will you?

RALPH   We were just wondering how we could cheer up Dorcas's thing.

ABIGAIL   Stafford? Oh, I wouldn't bother. (*She holds out the scarf*)

Ralph comes down the slope slightly to take it

How are you feeling, Pa?

RALPH   Oh, I'm perfectly fine.

ABIGAIL   Are you?

RALPH   I'm sad your mother's gone. I mean, it wasn't a surprise. We all knew it was going to happen sooner or later but all the same, it's sad. (*Pause*) I'll say this though, now we're alone. If you get one quarter the happiness out of your marriages – or your relationships or what-have-yous – if you get one quarter what your mother and I had, then I'll envy you.

DORCAS   You can never guarantee it.

RALPH   It entirely depends what you both put into it.

DORCAS   Aha.

ABIGAIL (*drily*) With strong emphasis on the 'both'.

Melvyn appears at the top. Brenda is still in tow

MELVYN Dad, is that St Mary's Church spire or Pendon Church?

RALPH (*to the girls*) You take a tip from that one. He knows what he's about. Don't you?

MELVYN What?

RALPH (*reclimbing the slope*) Where's Pendon Church supposed to be?

MELVYN Over there behind us.

RALPH Not unless it's been moved. You ought to know that. You're looking north-west that way. Pendon'll be over there.

Ralph, Melvyn and Brenda go off

Abigail and Dorcas are alone

ABIGAIL Was this really where we came for picnics? I suppose it was, just I remember it as much bigger.

An impatient car horn sounds

ABIGAIL (*calling*) All right. My husband is at his worst today. It is my mother's funeral and all he can think about is his bloody meeting. I don't know how long I can cope. I honestly don't. (*Indicating Ralph*) It's all right for him and his 'what you put into it'. I've flung the lot in and it's disappeared without trace.

DORCAS You shouldn't have given up your job.

ABIGAIL We can't have Mrs Smythe working, can we? That won't do.

DORCAS We're going to have to sort Pa out, you know.

ABIGAIL (*abstracted*) Oh yes.

DORCAS I mean, if in the long run we consider it best that I come home and look after him . . .

ABIGAIL Well, we'll see, shall we?

DORCAS   I hastily add I don't want to. I love him. But not that much. It's taken me a hell of a long time to get where I am and unless I have to . . .

ABIGAIL   No, well, don't.

DORCAS   I mean, I've got my own programme now, you know.

ABIGAIL   Yes.

DORCAS   Twice a week.

ABIGAIL   Yes.

DORCAS   Half-an-hour.

ABIGAIL   Super.

DORCAS   Well . . .

ABIGAIL   Do people listen? I mean . . .

DORCAS   (*flaring*) Yes, they do listen. Thousands of people listen. Do you have any idea of the daytime listening figures for local radio?

ABIGAIL   O.K., O.K.

DORCAS   Well, it's a lot of people. A lot of people listen to radio. I know you don't.

ABIGAIL   I don't. Well, I can never find anything on our radio. Except cricket or German stations. Mind you, ours is so complicated. You press buttons and all sorts of lights flash on and off and then Germans start talking in the bathroom . . . (*Slight pause*) Don't worry about Pa. We'll keep an eye on him. I'll keep an eye on him.

DORCAS   That's right. We used to toboggan down this slope. It all comes back to me now.

ABIGAIL   Stafford seems his usual jolly self.

DORCAS   Oh yes. There are problems. I think I've found a way to use him on my programme anyway. That'll help. You know, book reviewing and the odd interview. Could help his confidence. Mind you, he's not at his best today. He doesn't approve of all this, you see.

ABIGAIL   What, you mean the funeral?

DORCAS   No. He came along but he deliberately refused to go into the church for the service.

ABIGAIL   Didn't he come in? I never noticed.

DORCAS No, I don't think anyone noticed. Except me. That's why he's upset, really. I mean, what's the point of standing outside in a freezing churchyard for hours on end if no-one notices. I suppose God might have done.

ABIGAIL And Mother.

DORCAS She'll have laughed.

ABIGAIL So would God, I should think. Are you going to marry this Stafford man?

DORCAS No.

ABIGAIL Thank goodness.

DORCAS He doesn't believe in marriage either.

Patrick returns

PATRICK (*genially*) Just to say quickly – sorry to interrupt – just to say cheerio, love, see you later on tonight.

ABIGAIL What are you doing?

PATRICK I'm going. I said two forty-five. It is now two fifty. We're in injury time and I'm off.

ABIGAIL Patrick, you cannot leave us here.

PATRICK Sorry. I did say.

ABIGAIL You realize people are going to have to walk home?

PATRICK Sorry.

Patrick goes

ABIGAIL Patrick! God, the bastard. Patrick! The b-a-s-t . . . Now what are we going to do?

DORCAS Walk, I suppose. (*Calling*) Pa! Pa, we're going . . .

ABIGAIL I'll see if I can stop him.

Abigail goes out after Patrick

DORCAS (*calling*) Pa.

Simon appears at the top of the hill

SIMON Hallo. Want some help?

DORCAS No, it's all right. Could you just hurry them up, please.

SIMON   (*coming down the slope*) Right. They're just coming. Been a slight mishap.

DORCAS   What's happened?

SIMON   Nothing much. Your aunt's fallen down a hole, actually.

DORCAS   God.

SIMON   Quite a small one. She's a bit shaken up, that's all. (*Waving car keys*) I said I'd get her boot from the stick. Or rather her stick from the boot. Excuse me (*He turns to go*)

Abigail returns, almost colliding with Simon

Excuse me. Just getting the . . .

Simon waves the keys and goes

ABIGAIL   Well, Pat's gone. He's driven off, nearly running me over in the process. In films, if the wife jumps out in front of the car waving her arms, the husband generally pulls up with a scream of brakes. Patrick accelerates and drives straight at me.

DORCAS   How many does Len's car hold? Five at pinch, I reckon. That's Len, Auntie Rita, Pa and two others. The rest of us can walk.

ABIGAIL   I'm not walking. Not in these shoes. It's miles.

DORCAS   Well, all right. You and Brenda go. We'll start walking and Len can come back for us.

ABIGAIL   That's if we can prise Brenda away from Melvyn for that long. God, she's a dreary girl. I tried to talk to her in the car. Everything I said – (*imitating Brenda*) – gneeer.

DORCAS   (*similarly*) Gneeer.

ABIGAIL   She'll have to go. I mean, Melvyn is not getting stuck with that.

DORCAS   The main worry is she's stopped him doing any work. If he doesn't get his exams this summer, they'll sling him out of Medical School.

ABIGAIL   She'll have to go.

DORCAS   Gneeer.

Stafford comes stamping down the slope

Are they coming?

STAFFORD   Stupid old bag's fallen down a hole.

ABIGAIL   Who has?

DORCAS   Rita. She's O.K.

STAFFORD   My shoes are leaking.

DORCAS   Good, it'll wash your feet. Did you push her?

STAFFORD   Who?

DORCAS   Auntie Rita.

STAFFORD   No, her fascist husband, wasn't it?

ABIGAIL   Len pushed her?

STAFFORD   The fascist.

DORCAS   Well, I've got some wonderful news for you. You're going to have to walk home now.

STAFFORD   (*appalled*) Walk?

ABIGAIL   Yes. That other great fascist, my husband, has gone off in his car.

STAFFORD   (*stamping off*) Oh, Jesus.

Simon enters with Rita's walking stick, almost colliding with Stafford

SIMON   Whoops, sorry, old boy.

DORCAS   You're very athletic.

SIMON   I'm very out of training. Your husband's car's gone, did you know?

ABIGAIL   Yes, thank you.

SIMON   Oh. Oh well. Walk'll do us good, won't it? Shan't be a tick.

Simon bounds up the slope with great ease, and is gone

ABIGAIL   Well, say what you like about Brenda . . .

DORCAS   Gneeer.

ABIGAIL   Her brother's a bit of all right, isn't he? Where did she find him? I didn't even know she had a brother.

DORCAS   Apparently he's been abroad till recently. Africa.

ABIGAIL   What is he? An oil man?

12

DORCAS   No. Machinery, I think he said.

ABIGAIL   Oh. Married, of course?

DORCAS   No. Divorced, apparently.

ABIGAIL   Oh.

DORCAS   He's quite nice, isn't he? I mean, he tends to call you 'old bean' a bit. I suppose that comes of living in Africa.

ABIGAIL   How come you know him and I don't?

DORCAS   Well, he's a great friend of Mel's and – um – you don't get invited to Christmas dances at the rugger club, do you?

ABIGAIL   What, with Patrick? He faints at the sight of a goal post. Does Simon play?

DORCAS   Yes. Wing forward.

ABIGAIL   Is that good?

DORCAS   Tough.

ABIGAIL   God. No wonder Stafford's sulking.

DORCAS   How do you mean?

ABIGAIL   If he thinks he's competing with that.

DORCAS   Rubbish.

ABIGAIL   How do you mean?

DORCAS   What I say. Mind your own business. Rubbish.

ABIGAIL   What have I said?

DORCAS   Keep your nose out.

Abigail looks at her

ABIGAIL   Oooo-hoooo-hoooo. (*Slyly*) Toss you for him then.

DORCAS   Don't be childish, Abigail, be your age.

ABIGAIL   Oooo-hoooo-hoooo.

DORCAS   (*a little hot and embarrassed*) I'm going to find Stafford.

Dorcas goes towards the car

Abigail pulls a face

After a moment Simon appears at the top of the slope

SIMON   (*smiling at Abigail*) Hallo.

ABIGAIL   (*with new charm*) Hallo.

13

SIMON They're all coming. She's able to walk.

ABIGAIL Oh good.

Ralph appears, with Rita and Len following behind

RALPH What's that Patrick doing, driving off like that?

ABIGAIL I'm sorry, Pa, he couldn't wait.

RALPH Well, someone's going to have to walk and it won't be me. (*Descending the slope*) Rita's fallen down again.

ABIGAIL Yes, I heard she had.

RALPH I think she drinks, you know.

ABIGAIL No, she doesn't. It's your fault, Pa, you shouldn't take her up hills.

RALPH (*ignoring this*) Anyway, the first fine day we have this year and there probably won't be more than one anyway, we're going to have a picnic. That's settled.

RITA (*descending the slope*) Carefully, now, carefully.

LEN All right. Let me take the weight, let me take the weight.

RALPH How many can your car hold, Len?

LEN Four. Not more than four. The springs won't take it.

RALPH How many of us are there, then?

ABIGAIL Nine. There must be nine of us now Patrick's gone.

LEN He's a big help, he is.

SIMON I've said I don't mind walking at all.

RALPH Splendid. That makes eight, then.

LEN You're going to have to take another look at this knee, Ralph.

RALPH Yes, with the greatest of pleasure but not in the middle of a field.

Melvyn and Brenda emerge from the top of the slope and start down. Simultaneously, Dorcas returns from the direction of the road

DORCAS Stafford's not waiting. He's gone. He's going to hitch back to the village.

RALPH Splendid. Now we're seven. Any more volunteers?

MELVYN We'll walk.

RALPH Good lad.

MELVYN You don't mind walking, do you, Bren?

BRENDA   No.

ABIGAIL   (*sotto voce*) Gneeer.

LEN   They shouldn't be there, those holes up there, you know.

RITA   Those holes.

LEN   I think they've been dug maliciously. I'm going to have a quiet word about this in the right ear.

RITA   In the right ear.

LEN   I mean, if Rita had fallen badly, this would have been very serious.

RITA   Very serious.

Len and Rita go to the car

RALPH   (*making to follow them*) We'll be waiting in the car, you lot. You sort it out between you. One spare seat going. That's all. You used to toboggan down that slope, you know, Dorcas. Do you remember that?

DORCAS   Yes, Pa.

RALPH   Yes. (*He gazes at the slope*) I'm glad we stopped, you know. I couldn't have gone home straightaway.

Ralph leaves

Slight pause

MELVYN   Well, we'll be starting off then.

ABIGAIL   Yes, yes. We'll catch you up.

DORCAS   No, Abi, you're going in the car.

ABIGAIL   No, no, you go.

DORCAS   Don't be silly.

ABIGAIL   No, please.

DORCAS   But you said just now . . .

ABIGAIL   No – no – please. You go.

Slight pause

MELVYN   Well, see you there.

ABIGAIL   Yes.

DORCAS   Yes.

SIMON   Cheers, Mel. Bren.

15

Melvyn and Brenda go

Well . . .

DORCAS   Now, for goodness sake, this is stupid. Abi, please
. . .

ABIGAIL   No, honestly.

DORCAS   (*getting meaner*) Abi.

ABIGAIL   What?

DORCAS   Simon, tell her to go in the car.

SIMON   Well . . .

DORCAS   Simon . . .

SIMON   Er . . .

Slight pause

DORCAS   Oh, this is stupid. I mean, it's just stupid. There is
no point in the three of us walking. I mean, it's miles. It's
stupid. It'll take hours.

ABIGAIL   Quite.

SIMON   Well, why don't I go in the car? (*He laughs*)

*Dorcas and Abigaïl look at him amused. He stops laughing. A distant
car horn is heard*

Well . . . Tell you what, why don't you toss for it?

ABIGAIL   Why not?

DORCAS   (*reluctantly*) All right.

SIMON   O.K. (*Producing a coin*) Easy solution. Call. (*He tosses*)

ABIGIAL   Heads.

*Simon has tossed in the manner of all good sporting referees. The coin
lands in the grass. Abigail and Dorcas move to examine it. They look
at each other. Depending on the result, either prearranged but preferably
random, one of them moves towards the car*

ABIGAIL
or   } O.K. See you back there, then.
DORCAS

SIMON   Yes, right. See you. 'Bye. Think of us.

   One sister leaves

A pause. Simon scoops up the coin. The sound of the car departing is heard

   Right. Here we go. Best foot forward, eh?

ABIGAIL
or   }Yes ...
DORCAS

   They go out

The Lights fade

Depending on who leaves with Simon, either Abigail or Dorcas, either Scene 2 Abigail or Scene 2 Dorcas follows

Act One

Scene 2   *Abigail*

The same. A bright, sunny Sunday afternoon in June

Stafford enters, carrying a car rug and the Sunday papers. He throws the rug down, sits on it and starts to read. Dorcas enters after a moment, bearing picnic baskets and paraphernalia

DORCAS   God, I wish there was a way we could park nearer. That car's overheating. (*She dumps down the gear*) Stafford, you have carried precisely nothing.

STAFFORD   (*swatting about him*) Bloody wasps.

DORCAS   You're useless, Stafford. What are you, you're useless. I have to do everything, don't I?

STAFFORD   (*unmoved by this*) You're bigger than me.

DORCAS   No sign of the others. Stafford . . .

STAFFORD   (*reading*) Uh?

DORCAS   You're going to have to try and join in a bit today.

STAFFORD   (*looking up*) Join in?

DORCAS   When the others arrive, when the picnic starts.

STAFFORD   (*alarmed*) Join in what?

DORCAS   Conversation, Stafford. Chitter chatter. Social niceties.

STAFFORD   God.

DORCAS   Like talking to my father. When he asks after you, you do not turn your back or bury your head and particularly you don't walk away.

STAFFORD   Walk away? When did I walk away?

DORCAS   Always. Always you're walking away. As soon as anyone says anything to you that you don't particularly like the sound of. I mean, unless there really is something wrong with you . . .

STAFFORD   There's nothing wrong with me.

DORCAS   Well then.

18

STAFFORD It just so happens I am that rare being, someone who doesn't automatically and egocentrically want to be the continual centre of attention.

DORCAS Oh, cobblers.

STAFFORD Eh?

DORCAS Of course you do. What else do you think you want?

STAFFORD What?

DORCAS That's exactly what you want to be. By deliberately walking away from the centre of things, you're merely trying to draw attention to yourself thus making yourself the centre of attention which is all you wanted in the first place.

STAFFORD I . . . Oh – God. (*He walks away*)

DORCAS There you go.

STAFFORD (*snarling*) What now?

DORCAS You're walking away.

STAFFORD (*flinging himself down*) Oh.

DORCAS What are you, Stafford? You're useless.

STAFFORD Look, I'm a poet. I'm a writer. I'm not a Knights-bridge socialite.

DORCAS Fine. Then be a poet, Stafford. Only in that case, let's at least see or hear some poetry.

STAFFORD It's just, you know . . . With you, it's fine. It's when I get among people. You know?

DORCAS Yes, I know.

STAFFORD I let you down, didn't I? I let you down with the B.B.C. job. I blew it.

DORCAS It doesn't matter.

STAFFORD It matters to me. You gave me that chance and I blew it. You're a rock, kid. No-one else has helped me like you have. I rely on you, Dorc. Do you know that?

DORCAS Yes.

STAFFORD Do you mind? Me relying on you?

DORCAS No. That's all right.

STAFFORD It's all right?

DORCAS Only . . .

STAFFORD What?

DORCAS Well, there are just occasions, Staff, I mean, only once in a very blue moon when I need someone to prop me up for a change.

STAFFORD (*considering this*) Yes. I see that, I see that. I'm getting it together. Just give me time, Dorc.

Melvyn and Brenda enter. He carries the rest of the picnic gear. She carries a stunter kite, still in its box, and the kite string separately

MELVYN Here you are. I locked the car.

DORCAS Dump them there. (*She indicates the spot where she has put the other gear*) Any sign of the others?

MELVYN No, not yet. If they've gone by way of the cemetery they won't be here for a bit. Not with Len driving at four miles an hour.

DORCAS The regular weekly visit. Well, we finally made it. Perfect day. Not even Rita can complain.

MELVYN Is Abi coming?

DORCAS Abi probably, yes. But who with is anyone's guess.

MELVYN Ah. (*He does not care to pursue that*) Brought the kite.

DORCAS Oh yes.

MELVYN (*taking it from Brenda*) Look, you see, it's a stunter.

DORCAS Oh yes. All right, Brenda?

BRENDA I'm all right.

DORCAS Good. Not keeping Mel from his studies too much, are you?

BRENDA What?

MELVYN She's not.

DORCAS Sure?

MELVYN Don't keep on at her, Dorc.

DORCAS I'm not.

MELVYN Yes, you are.

DORCAS (*shrugging*) All right. It's just you've got exams in a few days, haven't you?

MELVYN Yes, all right.

Abigail appears at the top of the slope

ABIGAIL   Hallo.

DORCAS   Good lord, hallo. Where did you spring from?

ABIGAIL   Oh, I've been here some time.

DORCAS   Have you? Where did you park your car?

ABIGAIL   I didn't bring it.

DORCAS   Oh.

ABIGAIL   I cycled.

MELVYN   Cycled?

ABIGAIL   Yes.

DORCAS   You cycled?

ABIGAIL   Yes.

DORCAS   All alone?

ABIGAIL   Yes. Most of the way.

DORCAS   Ah.

ABIGAIL   Yes.

Slight pause

  Simon appears at the top of the slope

SIMON   Ah, hallo.

DORCAS   (*heartily*) Hallo.

MELVYN   Hallo.

SIMON   Smashing day.

DORCAS   Yes.

SIMON   (*after a slight pause*) What have you got there? Is it a kite?

MELVYN   Yeah. Brand new. Bought it yesterday.

SIMON   Looks a good one.

MELVYN   Have you flown this sort?

SIMON   I have done.

MELVYN   Stunters?

SIMON   Yes.

MELVYN   Great.

Pause

ABIGAIL   My old bike's still marvellous, you know. We – I

21

mean, I got it out of the garage and I oiled the chain and I gave it a good clean up – and things. And it's as good as new. I'm going to ache like hell tomorrow though.

DORCAS   Yes, I wouldn't be surprised.

SIMON   Well.

Slight pause. Suddenly, Brenda is galvanized into action

BRENDA   Yeeeow – wur – wur – wur – yow – wow – wow . . . .

DORCAS   What on earth's the matter?

MELVYN   It's all right, it's all right.

BRENDA   It's a wasp, it's a wasp.

MELVYN   It's gone, it's gone, it's all right.

BRENDA   Wur – wur . . .

MELVYN   (*soothingly*) It's all right, calm down. It's gone. (*To the others*) She doesn't like wasps.

DORCAS   Yes.

SIMON   Well, shall we fly it now or after tea?

MELVYN   Well, now, if you like.

SIMON   There's a bit of breeze up there. They need a bit of wind, you see, these stunters. It's the type with twin lines, I take it?

MELVYN   Yes, right. Are they difficult to handle?

SIMON   No, not really. I mean, only if the wind's very strong and then they're all over the place. (*Starting to climb the slope*) No, I've seen experts handling five or six at once.

MELVYN   (*following with Brenda*) What, flying in formation?

SIMON   Right. Will you excuse us? We're just going kite flying. (*He gives Abigail a swift one-armed hug and a kiss on the cheek*) Won't be long.

ABIGAIL   Right.

Simon goes off with Melvyn and Brenda

Abigail attempts to meet Dorcas's stare

Pa gone to the cemetery first, has he?

DORCAS   Apparently.

ABIGAIL   The Sunday ritual.

DORCAS   Yes.

STAFFORD   (*with a suppressed snarl of rage at what he is reading*) Gurrrrr!

ABIGAIL   What's the matter with him?

DORCAS   Nothing. He's reading the Sunday papers. He always does that. Take no notice (*Moving slightly away from Stafford*) Haven't seen you for a bit.

ABIGAIL   No. Well, I've been – er . . .

DORCAS   Yes.

ABIGAIL   Tell me, how does Pa seem to you these days? I mean, you see him less than I do so it's probably more noticeable to you. It's difficult for me to tell – seeing him, what, two or three times a week. He does seem to me to be getting – well – a bit odd. Do you find that?

DORCAS   He's always rather odd.

ABIGAIL   Yes. He keeps telling me he's seen Mother.

DORCAS   He's told me that, too.

ABIGAIL   And sometimes, if you turn up unexpectedly, you can hear him talking to her in the other room.

DORCAS   He may be talking to himself.

ABIGAIL   No, no. The other day I heard him telling her a funny story. Roaring with laughter. Him that is. And then there's some days he refuses to wear socks and at least once a week he wants his bed moving round because of the way the earth's rotating. I mean, he can't be se-nile, can he, not yet? He's not old enough. He's only just seventy. (*She reflects*) That reminds me, it's his birthday soon.

DORCAS   I don't know why he gave up his practice. At least he met a lot of people.

ABIGAIL   Perhaps it's a good job he did. Otherwise he might have had all his patients shifting their beds about in their bare feet. Oh well, he's harmless at the moment. (*Slight pause*) How are you?

DORCAS   Not so bad.

23

ABIGAIL   (*nodding towards Stafford*) Things still all right with huh-huh?

DORCAS   Chugging on.

ABIGAIL   I see.

DORCAS   That's about all you can say. I shan't ask about you.

ABIGAIL   No.

DORCAS   You don't find it a problem?

ABIGAIL   No. (*Slight pause*) Yes. I don't know. (*In a sudden outburst*) I'm sorry, Dorc, but I'm having a marvellous time. I know it sounds immature and adolescent to say it but he's just an amazing, super, wonderful, sexy, understanding man.

DORCAS   Oh, goodo.

ABIGAIL   And I'm incredibly happy.

Pause

DORCAS   Is Patrick happy too?

ABIGAIL   Oh, don't go and spoil it by mentioning Patrick.

DORCAS   I'm sorry. I'm afraid I'm out of touch with all this. I take it Patrick knows?

ABIGAIL   I suppose he does. He's not a fool. I've never told him officially. We haven't discussed Simon. But then we don't discuss anything anyway. Unless it appears on Patrick's official breakfast time agenda. And that consists mainly of food. Minutes of the last meal and proposals for the next.

DORCAS   Are you planning to leave him?

ABIGAIL   I might. I don't know. I honestly don't know. Simon wants me to, of course. But . . .

DORCAS   You'd be giving up a lot.

ABIGAIL   Hah . . .

DORCAS   Of course you would.

ABIGAIL   Perhaps. But look what I'd be getting.

DORCAS   In other words, you're still not fully committing yourself to Simon yet?

ABIGAIL   No. Not fully. (*Suspiciously*) Why?

DORCAS   No reason.

Slight pause

ABIGAIL (*happily*) Oh, Dorc, you just don't know.
DORCAS No. True enough.

Stafford comes across another offensive paragraph

STAFFORD (*groaning*) Gaaaarrrrrrr!
DORCAS Still, while a girl has Stafford, things can't be all bad.
ABIGAIL Is that permanent now?
DORCAS No.
ABIGAIL Why not?
DORCAS I don't think that's practical. Not with Stafford. Unless I legally adopt him. I suppose that would make it permanent.
ABIGAIL You don't hate me, do you? It was really only luck, wasn't it? I mean, that day. It could just as easily have been you and Simon. And if it had been the other way round, I would've – I *would* have been. I promise. Thrilled. Delighted.

Brenda enters down the slope

BRENDA It's flying, it's flying. Look.
DORCAS Oh yes.
ABIGAIL Wheee!
BRENDA (*going to her handbag, as she passes Stafford*) It's so pretty. Look, look.
STAFFORD Fantastic.
BRENDA It's really lovely.
DORCAS (*to Abigail*) Well, until you've decided, please for God's sake don't let Pa hear about it.
ABIGAIL Of course not.
DORCAS He's very fond of you and Patrick. And I'd keep it from Uncle Len as well, unless you want it splashed all over the front of the Police Gazette.
BRENDA Simon, can I have a go? Please, please.

Brenda runs off

ABIGAIL   Now, there's a more urgent problem.

DORCAS   What?

ABIGAIL   That. (*She nods in Brenda's direction*)

DORCAS   Oh, that. Gneeer.

ABIGAIL   I mean, dear brother's more infatuated than ever. And she gets more horrific each day. Well, I've done my bit. He won't listen to me. I've tried.

DORCAS   I think it's a lost cause.

ABIGAIL   She'll trap him into marriage eventually. She's the type. Poor kid. I mean, he knows nothing. She'll destroy the boy. We can't let that happen, can we?

ABIGAIL   Gneer.

DORCAS   Gneer.

Simon and Brenda come on. Brenda holds the two control lines to an invisible kite somewhere off. She grips the plastic handles tied to the lines. Simon, behind her, attempts to guide her actions by guiding her wrists

SIMON   Now, keep it steady. Keep it steady. Now, pull on your left. Pull on your left. Left, left, left.

BRENDA   (*very excited*) I am, I am.

SIMON   This is your left. This one. Pull.

BRENDA   I'm pulling.

SIMON   Look out, it's going to hit the tree. Let me take it, let me take it.

MELVYN   (*off*) It's going to hit the tree.

BRENDA   It's terribly difficult.

SIMON   That's it, I've got it, I've got it. There she goes.

MELVYN   (*off, distant*) Well done.

ABIGAIL   Oh, look at that. Isn't that marvellous? Wheee! That's brilliant, Simon.

SIMON   Want a go?

ABIGAIL   Isn't it difficult?

SIMON   No, not at all.

BRENDA   (*running off to rejoin Melvyn*) Don't believe him. It's terribly difficult.

Brenda goes

SIMON (*enveloping Abigail between his arms to allow a take-over of the controls*) Now, here. Take the lines. That's it, one in each hand. Now, you pull that and it goes that way . . .

ABIGAIL Wheee.

SIMON And that makes it go that way.

ABIGAIL Wheee . . .

SIMON With a bit of practice, you can do that.

ABIGAIL Wheee!

SIMON That's it. Let it come back.

ABIGAIL Fun!

SIMON Otherwise you'll lose the wind. It's too sheltered down here, you see.

ABIGAIL Wheeee! Look, Dorc, isn't this marvellous?

DORCAS Yes.

Brenda screams, off

ABIGAIL (*calling off*) Look out!

MELVYN (*off, distant*) Careful.

ABIGAIL Sorry. Whoops.

Abigail moves off, controlling the kite

Simon watches with a protective eye. Dorcas studies Simon. Stafford reads on doggedly

STAFFORD (*hurling the Colour Supplement from him*) Oh, Jesus (*To Dorcas*) A two-thousand-pound bathtub.

DORCAS What's that, love?

STAFFORD A bath costing two thousand pounds. I hope he drowns in it, the stupid bastard.

DORCAS Ah. (*She goes back to watching the kite*)

SIMON You going to have a go later?

DORCAS No, I don't think so. I don't think it's really me somehow.

SIMON There's nothing to it. Just a knack. Once you've got the hang of it, you're . . .

27

Abigail laughs, off

(*Watching the kite's manœuvres*) Hey! (*To Dorcas*) How are you keeping, then? Haven't seen you for a bit.

DORCAS Oh, I've been around.

SIMON Are you still doing your radio programme?

DORCAS Oh yes. Tuesdays and Thursdays.

SIMON Do you know, I've never managed to catch it. What's it about?

DORCAS Well, it varies. Depends what I feel like. It's a sort of general arts programme and then I play records and then people phone up. Mainly to complain.

SIMON About the records?

DORCAS No – well – sometimes. Mostly about roads and street lighting and should the Mayor have a car or a bicycle, that sort of thing.

SIMON Ah.

ABIGAIL (*off*) Ah!

SIMON Good lord, look at that! She's getting very good. (*Calling*) Well done.

DORCAS Are you in love with her?

SIMON Er – yes. Yes.

DORCAS Sorry.

SIMON No, no. Not at all, no. Yes, I do. I mean, I am. Yes.

DORCAS So you would like it to be permanent?

SIMON Well, from my side, yes. Naturally I can't speak for Abi, she's . . .

DORCAS It's a bigger decision, isn't it? For her.

SIMON Yes. (*He ponders*) How do you mean?

DORCAS Well, she'd be giving up quite a bit. Materially. Patrick's not poor. Let's be honest. It's a consideration. It has to be.

SIMON Oh yes, yes.

DORCAS I mean, God, we're adults. None of us are quite that naïve any more. To think we can live our lives on love. Like Melvyn.

SIMON   Or Brenda. Quite. No. I'm starting teaching again this autumn. I used to teach before I went abroad. P.E. and games, you know. Abi wants to get back to work again, too. She's been rusting away, you know. Terrible waste of a good brain.

DORCAS   Well, if that's what she wants.

SIMON   Yes. That's what she says she wants, anyway.

DORCAS   I just hope she doesn't finish up being hurt or disappointed. I mean, no criticism of you. One's seen it before, you see. When she married Patrick, she couldn't wait to give up her career. Become a home wife, a mother even – all things domestic. It was all she dreamed of. And now she wants out.

SIMON   Yes, but isn't that typical of all of us? Wanting what we haven't got. And then, once we get it . . .

Abigail laughs, off

(*Shouting*) Mind the trees! (*To Dorcas*) Don't worry. She won't be hurt. Not by me, anyway. And I'll do my best not to disappoint her.

DORCAS   That's not what I meant.

SIMON   I know. I know. I'm joking . . .

DORCAS   Abi's a person who expects rather a lot from life.

SIMON   Yes, yes. I do know.

DORCAS   She also expects a lot from people, too. And generally we let her down, I'm afraid. At least, she feels we have. In her eyes, that amounts to the same thing. Father, me – Mother, of course. And now Patrick. I think she feels we've all failed her somehow. The point is, I don't think her image of us was one we could possibly live up to. Let's face it, most of us are just ordinary people. Average. Like you and me.

SIMON   Yes. I think she's fond of me, though.

DORCAS   I'm sure she is.

SIMON   Has she said anything to you?

DORCAS   She doesn't say much to me.

SIMON   No . . . (*Looking back at Abigail*) She's a marvellous person, though.

DORCAS Oh yes. God, there's a lot to be said for idealists –
I'm not knocking them.

Abigail bounds into view, still holding on to the kite

ABIGAIL (*over her shoulder*) Were you watching?

SIMON Yes.

DORCAS Well done.

ABIGAIL It's hard work.

SIMON (*drawing further away from Abigail*) This disappointment
you say she feels with her relationships. Is it general or just
. . .

DORCAS Only the ones I've known, that's all.

ABIGAIL What are you two doing?

SIMON Just talking. (*Returning to Dorcas*) I mean, you could say
that's the same with a lot of people, couldn't you? It's not
that exceptional.

DORCAS Probably not. I don't know. I'm more misanthropic,
that's all. I don't expect anything much from anyone and
as a result, I'm frequently quite pleasantly surprised. It
probably means I'm lacking in imagination or something.

SIMON Not at all. I'm sure you're not.

DORCAS Well, it's nice of you to say so but I think I probably
am.

SIMON Now, you're not one of those people who continually
run themselves down, are you?

DORCAS How does it go? 'Look in thy glass and the face thou
viewest – Now is the time that face should form another.'

SIMON No, I don't know that one.

DORCAS From the sonnets, I think.

SIMON Aha, aha.

DORCAS Well, I suppose if one gets positively no encouragement after a bit it tends to happen. Particularly for a
woman.

SIMON Oh, come on. Don't give me that. No-one's ever
encouraged you at all?

DORCAS Not a lot.

ABIGAIL (*still struggling with the kite but trying to get a better look*)
Can someone take over now, please?

DORCAS Women are very realistic, you know. We acknowledge our faults pretty early in life. We have to, to conceal
them. I mean, I know I'm not beautiful in the conventional
sense.

SIMON Now, I must stop you there. What do you mean by
convention? What is a convention? It's something man-
made, surely.

DORCAS Yes, and as a man you're necessarily ruled by them,
aren't you? Like all men, you're a slave to convention.

ABIGAIL I can't hold this thing much longer. I'm going to let
go.

SIMON No, I don't accept that. That I'm conventional. I
mean, I like to think of myself as something more than that.

DORCAS All right, then, stop beating about the bush, be
perfectly honest. In the face of all that preconditioning, all
that male-oriented propaganda to which you've been
subjected from childhood upwards, can you honestly
describe me as a beautiful ... No, that's too unfair, I'll
rephrase that – as an attractive woman?

ABIGAIL Look, will somebody take this bloody kite?

SIMON (*laughing, confident now*) Well, I'm very sorry, young
woman, but I'm about to upset every preconception you've
ever had. I'm sorry to shatter all your myths about men but
it so happens that I do consider you to be an extremely
attractive woman. No – to hell with it – a beautiful woman.
And may I add by way of a bonus, quite fancy-able.

Abigail releases the kite

ABIGAIL Right. I have let it go.

DORCAS Thank you.

SIMON My pleasure.

ABIGAIL (*slithering down the bank to join them*) Hallo.

SIMON Oh, hallo. What have you done with the kite?

ABIGAIL I let it go.

SIMON   Oh, for God's sake, Abi, what did you do that for? Why?

DORCAS   She probably got bored with it.

Melvyn appears on the brow of the hill

MELVYN   Oy, you let go of it.

ABIGAIL   Sorry.

Brenda enters and joins Melvyn

MELVYN   It's all tangled up in the tree, now.

BRENDA   (*examining her bare foot*) I've got a splinter.

ABIGAIL   Sorry. Couldn't be helped.

SIMON   I'll come and help, Mel.

MELVYN   (*looking out from the vantage point of the bank*) Hey, there's a car just arrived.

DORCAS   Oh, they're here. We'd better get things organized. Mel, can you see if they want anything carrying?

ABIGAIL   (*sittting up*) Whose is it?

MELVYN   I think it's yours, Abi. Yes, it is, it must be ... (*Realizing*) Oh.

ABIGAIL   (*with a look of hatred at Dorcas*) You little sod.

DORCAS   What?

Patrick enters, quite at ease. Although in his Sunday gear, he still appears more formal than anyone else

PATRICK   Afternoon, all.

SIMON   Ah, hallo.

PATRICK   Hallo. (*Nodding to Abigail*) Hallo, dear.

ABIGAIL   Hallo, dear.

DORCAS   Did you say the kite was caught in a tree, Mel?

MELVYN   (*still staring*) Yep. (*Taking the hint*) Oh yes, right.

DORCAS   I'll give you a ...

MELVYN   Yes, thank you, would you ...?

Melvyn goes

DORCAS   Not at all. (*Hurrying up the bank*) See you in a minute.

Dorcas goes

PATRICK   (*beaming at them*) Surely.

Patrick gives Stafford a glance but Stafford remains unmoving and, as far as we can tell, unaware

Well, now, what's all this then?

SIMON   (*defensively*) What?

PATRICK   A secret picnic, is it? Everyone invited except me. That's a bit secretive, isn't it? I might have missed out. If someone hadn't told me.

ABIGAIL   Who told you?

PATRICK   A little bird.

ABIGAIL   I see. I didn't think you liked picnics.

PATRICK   Me? How little you know of me. I adore them. I never miss out on a picnic if I can possibly avoid it. Hallo, Simon, you're looking very fit. Don't you think so, Abi? You're looking marvellous. Terribly muscular. Just the sort of chap to have around in a tight picnic, eh?

Simon laughs rather nervously

Don't like the look of those clouds. Could be a bit of rain about later. How did you get here, Abi? Did you walk?

ABIGAIL   No, I came by bike.

PATRICK   Really? You mean, the old one in the garage? I thought that had seized up solid. Well, well. You come by car, Simon?

SIMON   By bike as well, actually.

PATRICK   Both on bikes. Coincidence. How splendidly healthy. Not the same bike, I take it?

Patrick laughs. The others do not

I'm ashamed to say I came in the Merc. Isn't that terrible? Perhaps I should take up cycling. It's obviously the way to meet people. Now, how do we intend to sort this one out? Any ideas?

33

ABIGAIL   There's nothing we can do this afternoon. Father will be arriving at any moment. Not to mention Uncle Len. Or Auntie Rita.

PATRICK   Well, something's going to have to be decided soon, darling, for all our sakes. Much as I admire this Spartan flurry of cycling and kite-flying, someone somewhere's got to give up with good grace, don't you think?

SIMON   I think it's rather up to Abi to choose who that's going to be, don't you?

PATRICK   Well, that's a point of view. She's not at her best as a decision-maker, you know. She does tend to become easily confused. Her eyes being bigger than her stomach. Or hadn't you noticed that about her?

SIMON   (*tensely*) No, I can't say I had. She always strikes me as being perfectly capable. As a woman, she seems to me to . . .

ABIGAIL   Would you both mind not talking about me in the third person?

PATRICK   Sorry, darling. She gets like this sometimes.

ABIGAIL   I am warning you, Patrick . . .

PATRICK   Splendid. We'll leave it to Abi then, shall we? Can't say fairer than that.

SIMON   You're taking this very casually.

PATRICK   The point is, have I any choice? Supposing I get physical and threaten you. You'd knock me down without the slightest difficulty. Screaming my head off at you both will only weaken my case further and, as Abi will tell you, I'm not much good at begging. So I'll have to be content to wait for her decision, won't I? But I'll tell you this much. If, finally, she does decide to leave me for you then I promise you I shall prove to be an extremely bad loser. No proper sporting background, you see. I shall drag you both through the most public, most vicious, expensive divorce it is possible for man to devise. I shall fight you both every inch of the way and by the time I've finished with you, you'll probably have to sell both your bicycles. (*He moves away from them*)

ABIGAIL (*sotto voce*) What are we going to do?

SIMON To be perfectly honest, I don't really know. At this present moment, I have a strong urge to go over there, wrap both his legs round his neck and stick his suede shoes in his mouth. But I suppose that would only be termed a temporary solution.

ABIGAIL Yes.

SIMON So . . .

ABIGAIL (*tearfully*) It's always like this. He always manages to ruin everything.

SIMON Yes . . .

Melvyn appears over the hill. He carries the kite without its strings

MELVYN They've just arrived.

ABIGAIL Oh.

MELVYN (*to Abigail, crossly*) We had to cut the strings, you know.

Dorcas comes down the slope. Brenda appears behind her more slowly, still limping

DORCAS (*briskly*) All right, everyone. Now they've arrived may I remind you this is Father's afternoon. It has taken six months of planning and hours of preparation, so all hatchets buried, please.

PATRICK Of course, of course.

DORCAS You can kill each other later . . . (*She sees Ralph coming*) Hallo, Pa.

Ralph enters

RALPH At last, at last. (*Seeing Patrick*) Ah-ha, there he is. Now, if we hadn't dropped in on him on our way to the cemetery, do you know, Abi, this fellow of yours wouldn't have known there was a picnic at all. Why didn't you tell him, you silly bundle?

ABIGAIL (*smiling limply*) I thought he knew. I forgot.

PATRICK We were just laughing about it.

35

RALPH Scatterhead. She gets no better the older she gets, does she?

PATRICK No.

DORCAS Where do you want to sit, Father? (*She holds one of the chairs*)

RALPH Just where you are, my dearest, as long as it's out of the wind. Mel, boy, see if your Uncle Len needs a hand, will you?

Melvyn comes down the slope. Brenda limps after him

And there's your girl. How's she? Good lord, she looks as if she's gone lame. You'll have to put her down, Mel.

BRENDA I've got a splinter.

Melvyn goes off

RALPH Good girl, good girl. (*To Patrick*) Going to be a fine doctor one day, that boy, if he ever gets his exams. Ah, look who's here, it's – er . . .

SIMON Simon.

RALPH Simon. I didn't see you. This is nice. I didn't expect to see you.

SIMON Yes.

ABIGAIL Wasn't it extraordinary? I was cycling here and who should I run into, metaphorically, but Simon. So I said do come. And here he is.

RALPH And why not? I mean, he's nearly one of the family, isn't he?

ABIGAIL I beg your pardon?

RALPH Well, he's thingummy-tight's brother, isn't he? I mean, if she and Mel keep going on the way they are.

Dorcas positions a chair for Ralph

ABIGAIL Oh, I see.

RALPH (*to Dorcas*) No, not there, lumpkin. A bit further round. I don't want it blowing down my neck, do I?

Melvyn returns with a fishing stool and a rug

(*Sitting*) That's better. That's better. (*To Stafford*) Good afternoon to you.

Dorcas kicks Stafford

How are you?

STAFFORD Yes, thank you.

RALPH Splendid. Thank you, Mel. Is Len managing?

MELVYN Yeah. He's just padlocking up the hubcaps.

RALPH I was telling them, Mel. If you keep your nose in your books and don't spend every second of every day ogling what's'ername there, you'll be a very fine doctor.

MELVYN (*spreading out the rug for him and Brenda, unmoved*) Yeah.

RALPH (*without offence*) He doesn't listen to a blasted word I say, does he? Well, this is nice, isn't it? We'd better get our tea in before the rain, that's all.

DORCAS What rain?

RALPH Look over there. See those clouds? Well, twenty minutes they'll be overhead.

ABIGAIL Nonsense.

RALPH Betcha. Seen it before.

PATRICK (*to Abigail*) Why's he only got one sock on?

ABIGAIL God knows.

Rita comes on with more bags

RITA Here we are. I don't like the look of those clouds.

RALPH Over here, Rita. We've reserved you a spot over here.

RITA We've been locking the car.

Len enters with other picnickery

LEN Can't be too careful. Not these days.

RALPH Won't do to have a copper having his car nicked, will it?

LEN If I related to you the statistics regarding car thefts for one month in this area, it would horrify you.

RITA Horrify you.

LEN Horrify you. We don't release the true figures. The general public would panic.

RALPH Yes, yes.

ABIGAIL Hope my bike's all right.

LEN Locked it up, have you?

ABIGAIL No, it's just under a bush over there.

LEN It is quite within bounds that by the time you get back to it, they'll have stripped it of everything.

RITA Stripped it.

LEN Bell, gears, lights back and front, wheels, rear reflectors, both sets of brakes and the saddle.

RITA Rear reflectors.

LEN And if it's a lady's bike and you're out of luck, they'll be lying in wait to rape you as well.

ABIGAIL Oh terrific, thanks.

LEN Just a warning.

SIMON (gallantly) Don't worry, I'll – er – I'll . . .

PATRICK What's that?

SIMON Nothing.

RALPH What's he saying?

SIMON I'll – er – I'll be able to keep an eye on the bikes from here.

PATRICK Jolly good.

RALPH Splendid. What's he talking about?

BRENDA Ugh!

RALPH (to Brenda) Have you got that thing out of your foot yet?

BRENDA No.

RALPH Well, put your hoof in your mouth and suck it. Can you suck your foot?

BRENDA No.

RALPH Dear oh dear. (To Len) She can't be much fun, can she?

DORCAS He's going completely mad.

RALPH (sitting back, basking) Now isn't this the perfect spot? Didn't I tell you? What could be nicer.

38

LEN It's all right now in broad daylight, but I wouldn't care to be sitting up here like this in the middle of the night.

ABIGAIL Why?

LEN Let us just say it is a favourite haunt.

RITA Haunted?

LEN No, not haunted. I'm saying it is a haunt for certain undesirables who wish to practise unnatural practices.

MELVYN Unnatural practices?

LEN I'm saying no more.

MELVYN What unnatural practices?

LEN I think I've said enough on that subject. We shall catch up with them and then . . .

MELVYN (*to Brenda*) We must come up here at night.

LEN Now, don't be young, lad, don't be young. Be your age.

RALPH Come on, then. Let's eat before the rain.

Len sits on the stool

DORCAS It's not going to rain.

RALPH Wait and see. Wait and see.

RITA Are you all right on that stool, Len?

LEN Oh yes. Many an hour I've spent on this stool, watching the rod.

RITA (*sorting out the bags*) Now then.

RALPH Still fish, do you, Len?

LEN Not as much as I did. Not as much as I'd like to.

RITA He's no time, have you?

LEN Not any more.

RITA Now, what have we got in here?

DORCAS All right, now. Nobody jump about. Rita and I will organize this. Everyone just sit down.

RALPH Do you hear that everybody? Leave it to Dorcas. In this family, you know, Simon, when it comes to organization we all leave it to Dorcas.

SIMON Ah.

ABIGAIL (*muttering*) It's only because she won't let anyone else help.

RITA (*finding a polythene box*) Ah now, these are Stafford's specials.

ABIGAIL Even if they wanted to.

DORCAS (*putting four sandwiches – half rounds – out of the box on to a paper plate*) Those are Stafford's specials.

RALPH What's this? Who's getting special treatment?

DORCAS These are nut sandwiches for Stafford.

RALPH Nut?

DORCAS He's a vegetarian.

RALPH Poor chap.

DORCAS There you are, Stafford.

STAFFORD Right.

DORCAS (*handing Simon eight cardboard plates*) Simon, could you dish those out, please?

SIMON Certainly.

Simon hands out the eight cardboard plates, including one for himself. When he gets to Len, he runs out

RALPH (*watching Dorcas*) Len, who does she remind you of now? Dorcas? Who is it she's like now?

RITA Amy, isn't it?

LEN Amy? Just like her mother.

RALPH Amy. Look at her. Once she gets set on anything. You see, Abi's like me. We're the fly-by-nights. Hopping about from this to that. (*To Abigail*) Aren't you?

ABIGAIL That's absolutely untrue.

PATRICK I'm saying nothing.

DORCAS Ham sandwich, everyone? (*She starts to take them round, eight half rounds, avoiding Stafford*)

By the time she gets to Len, she's run out. Simon has just discovered the shortage of plates

SIMON Oh.

LEN What, no plate for me?

SIMON We seem to be a plate short.

DORCAS Oh hell, are we?

RITA   Ah well, we'll be one extra, won't we?

ABIGAIL   (*looking at Patrick*) Yes, we will.

PATRICK   All right, I'll go. I'll go.

RITA   No, no, it's not Patrick who's extra, it's – er – Simon, there. We didn't expect him, did we?

RALPH   Ah-ha, an extra body.

PATRICK   Better hand in your plate, old son.

SIMON   Yes, well. Right. There. (*He offers Len his plate*) I don't mind.

ABIGAIL   (*restraining him*) Oh, don't be stupid. We must have a spare plate somewhere.

DORCAS   Yes, there is.

PATRICK   No, no. Look. Here. Have half of mine. (*He tears his plate in half*) Share and share alike.

Simon glares at him, his fists bunching.

ABIGAIL   (*springing up*) Oh, for heaven's sake. If we go on at this rate, no-one's going to get anything to eat at all. For the love of Mike, let me help.

DORCAS   Abi, please.

Abigail snatches up Stafford's plate of sandwiches

ABIGAIL   Right. Come along, take one.

STAFFORD   Er . , .

ABIGAIL   Oh come along, Stafford, for heaven's sake. Before it rains.

STAFFORD   Yeah, I think those are . . .

ABIGAIL   There you are, one for you . . . (*She takes the sandwich off the plate and plonks it on to the rug*)

DORCAS   (*who is still handing out ham sandwiches*) Abigail, please don't. You'll only muddle things up.

ABIGAIL   We can't sit around any longer, darling, we're all starving. (*She hands Stafford's remaining three sandwiches to Patrick, Brenda and Melvyn*)

Len rises momentarily and moves to look at the car. Dorcas finishes handing out the ham sandwiches

41

DORCAS   I think there will be enough to go round, Rita.

RITA   (*who has been unpacking eight cheese and tomato sandwiches*)
I think we made a few extra. (*To Len*) What are you doing,
love?

LEN   Just checking the car.

RITA   Could you hand out these cheese and tomato, please,
Simon?

SIMON   A pleasure.

*Simon goes round handing out the cheese and tomato. Stafford, who has
only one sandwich left, takes one. Simon thus runs out early, omitting
Rita and Len. Abigail dumps Stafford's empty sandwich plate on the
grass and finds some cardboard cups which she unpacks. Dorcas undoes
two thermos flasks, one with orange and one with tea. Rita opens the
egg and tomato sandwiches*

LEN   (*returning, meanwhile, to Simon*) Rumour has it, you're an
athlete, young man.

SIMON   (*serving cheese and tomato*) Well, used to be.

LEN   Were you a runner, by any chance?

RALPH   Careful how you answer that question, Simon.

SIMON   Well, yes, I used to run a bit.

ABIGAIL   (*taking the egg and tomato from Rita*) What are these?

SIMON   I'm certainly not a sprinter.

RITA   Egg and tomato, those are.

ABIGAIL   Right.

LEN   Cross-country at all?

ABIGAIL   One for you. (*She slaps an egg and tomato on the rug next
to Stafford*)

SIMON   Well, a bit. Not recently.

RALPH   Ah-ha. Ah-ha.

*Abigail hands out egg and tomato to everyone else. She runs out as she
gets to Rita and Len*

SIMON   Why are you asking? Were you a runner?

LEN   Years ago. Years ago.

RALPH   He was very good.

42

RITA He ran for the Police.

DORCAS Right, how are we doing?

ABIGAIL We're doing fine.

DORCAS (*muttering*) I wish she'd leave things alone.

RITA (*handing her the final batch of sandwiches*) Sardine and cucumber.

Dorcas distributes these

LEN No, I organize the local cross-country derby once a year. It's a light-hearted jaunt but we usually get quite a good field.

RALPH Light-hearted, he says.

LEN We run it around here.

SIMON Sounds fun.

LEN I might persuade you to enter, then?

ABIGAIL Right. Anything else?

SIMON Well . . .

DORCAS No, thank you so much, Abi. Sit down.

SIMON I'll see.

RALPH You know, Len, I'd fancy him against Murphy, you know.

LEN Oh no, no. Nobody beats Murphy.

SIMON Murphy?

RALPH Young Constable Murphy. Finest runner I've seen for some time.

RITA Len's brought him on from nothing.

LEN No, he won't touch Murphy. Promise you that.

ABIGAIL What about drinks?

RITA It's all right, Abi. I'll do those.

LEN Well, it's not till September the eighth. You've plenty of time.

SIMON I might just be fit by then, I suppose.

RITA Now, hands up for tea. And who wants orange squash?

Everyone puts up their hand

That's one, two . . .

MELVYN Are we putting our hands up for tea or orange squash?

RITA This is for tea.

MELVYN Oh no, I don't want tea.

RITA Well, if you want orange squash – don't put your hand up. Put your hand down.

Melvyn and Brenda put their hands down. Dorcas starts pouring tea

PATRICK I'm sorry, what are we putting our hands up for then?

DORCAS Up for tea, down for orange squash.

RALPH I'm completely lost, I'll have both.

DORCAS You have tea, Pa. Here you are.

RALPH Ah-ha.

LEN Look, I don't want to spoil anything, but I've got nothing at all.

DORCAS You must have. Where's your plate gone?

LEN I've never had a plate.

ABIGAIL Come on, here you are. Here's a plate. Here (*She picks up Dorcas's plate from the rug, tipping off the contents*)

DORCAS Abi, don't do that.

LEN Thank you.

DORCAS Those are mine. Now they're full of grass.

ABIGAIL All this fuss over a plate.

PATRICK (*picking up Stafford's old plate*) There's another plate here.

DORCAS Well, where did that come from?

PATRICK No idea.

LEN Right, I now have a plate. Is there anything to put on it?

DORCAS Look, this is ridiculous. If you'd only . . . Why has nobody given Uncle Len anything?

RALPH Well, I'm all right. (*He starts to eat*)

DORCAS Someone's got more than they should have.

RITA (*taking over the tea duties*) Stafford, orange or tea?

STAFFORD Er – orange.

During the following, Rita serves everyone with drinks. By the finish, Len, Rita, Ralph, Abigail and Patrick have tea. Simon, Brenda, Melvyn, Dorcas and Stafford have orange squash

BRENDA   It's a funny sandwich this.

RALPH   What's that, my beautiful?

BRENDA   It's all sort of gritty this sandwich.

RALPH   Gritty, is it? Never mind, it's probably been dropped somewhere. It's good for you grit. They give it to hens.

BRENDA   Ugggh. (*She looks inside the sandwich*)

DORCAS   (*interrupting her count*) Just a minute. Brenda, what are you eating there?

STAFFORD   I think that's one of mine.

DORCAS   Is that a nut sandwich?

MELVYN   Yes, it looks like nut.

BRENDA   Nut, yes.

DORCAS   Then what are you doing eating nut? That's supposed to be for Stafford.

BRENDA   Well, I didn't know. Someone gave it to me.

DORCAS   Oh, this is ridiculous. If you'd only all listened – if we'd only done this properly . . .

RALPH   Now, come on, old lumpkin. It's all right.

DORCAS   It is not all right. It happens every bloody time we have a picnic.

PATRICK   All right, own up. Who's eating Stafford's nuts? Come on.

LEN   I'm not eating anything. I've only got a plate.

DORCAS   All right, all right. We'll have to go round. Everybody stop eating, please. Just for one minute. Now, Stafford, what have you got?

STAFFORD   Er . . .

Dorcas snatches Stafford's sandwiches from him

DORCAS   You've got a nut. That's a nut one. Good. (*She hands that back to him*) A cheese and tomato and an egg and tomato. I don't know what you're doing with these. (*She holds on to*

45

the egg and tomato and the cheese and tomato) Right, next. Simon?

SIMON Er – I've got a ham, an egg and tomato, a cheese and tomato and a cucumber and something.

DORCAS (*checking her own sandwiches*) Cucumber and sardine. That is correct. Good. That is what I've got.

PATRICK (*to Simon*) Well done.

DORCAS Next. Abi?

ABIGAIL Ditto.

DORCAS Are you sure?

ABIGAIL I said yes. Ditto.

DORCAS This is all your fault, you know. If you hadn't . . .

ABIGAIL My God, if we'd waited till you . . .

PATRICK (*riding over this*) Now then, I have a very interesting selection here. It could qualify me for a major prize. I have a ham, a half-eaten cheese and tomato, a totally eaten egg and tomato and you'd better take my word for, a sardine and cucumber that I don't much like the look of and a nut one that I don't want at any price.

DORCAS Right. Give me that nut one, please.

PATRICK It's all yours.

DORCAS Thank you. Melvyn?

MELVYN Cheese and tom., egg and tom., cue. and sard., one ham, one nut.

DORCAS Give me the nut.

MELVYN What do I get instead?

DORCAS Nothing. Brenda?

BRENDA The same as Melvyn.

DORCAS Right, give me the nut one, please.

BRENDA I can't.

DORCAS Why not?

BRENDA I've eaten most of it.

DORCAS Oh God, why the hell did you eat it? Here you are, Staff, here's two more.

STAFFORD Right.

DORCAS Pa, are you happy?

RALPH   Perfectly. I've come out of it very well. The god of sandwiches has smiled upon me.

RITA   Yes, I only seem to have two but . . .

DORCAS   (*handing her the couple she has taken from Stafford*) That's all right. You have these two. And then I think we're all right. Is everybody happy now?

LEN   No. I still have nothing to eat whatsoever.

DORCAS   (*snatching up her own sandwiches*) All right, all right. Have these . . .

LEN   No, those are yours. I can't . . .

DORCAS   Please, I insist. Have them. (*She thrusts the sandwiches at Len*)

LEN   Now, what are you going to . . .?

DORCAS   Eat them. (*She goes and sits on the rug*)

Slight pause

(*Muttering*) This is the last time, this is postively the last time . . .

Pause

RALPH   Well, we've beaten the rain.

RITA   Yes, they're coming closer.

RALPH   Told you so. Well, just to say thank you all for coming along and humouring me. I'm sure you've all got other things you'd far sooner be doing.

PATRICK   No, I'm sure we haven't. Have we?

ABIGAIL   No.

RALPH   I must say when I told Amy on Wednesday, she was very, very touched. She wanted me to thank you.

LEN   Ah.

RITA   Oh.

DORCAS   Good.

Pause

RALPH   And what's been happening to Stratford these days?

ABIGAIL   Where?

47

DORCAS Stafford, Father. He's called Stafford.

RALPH Stafford, I beg his pardon. I'm always getting him wrong, aren't I? I know he's a railway station. What did I call him once? Stoke, Staleybridge, something like that. How are things going? Still working for Dorcas?

STAFFORD No.

DORCAS No, unfortunately it didn't work out.

RALPH Why not?

DORCAS Well, actually, he got sacked.

RALPH Good lord, sacked? Did she sack you, this girl?

DORCAS No, of course I didn't. Vernon did.

RALPH Vernon?

DORCAS Vernon Bradshaw, the station manager. It's a long story.

MELVYN Were you sacked because of your politics, Staff?

STAFFORD Yeah.

DORCAS No, he wasn't. (*To Stafford*) You weren't.

MELVYN If they fired him because of his politics . . .

DORCAS They didn't. If you must know, he started a fight in the B.B.C. canteen over the price of salads. And he finished up punching a vision mixer from the Sports Unit. The man was off work for three days and Vernon has banned Stafford from the studios pending an enquiry. That's all there was to it.

RALPH Good lord. The things they get up to in the B.B.C., eh?

LEN Nothing would surprise me where the media are concerned.

RALPH Ah.

Slight pause. Mel kisses Brenda

STAFFORD You see, it's . . .

BRENDA Ooh!

RALPH She'll get terrible indigestion, Mel, if you do that to her while she's eating.

ABIGAIL Come on, Mel, knock it off.

MELVYN All right.

PATRICK Otherwise we'll all start.

STAFFORD (*speaking softly and nervously*) It's – er – to do basi-
cally with more than just that . . .

DORCAS What are you saying, Staff? (*She signals for him to speak
up*)

*Stafford speaks again a little louder, but not loud enough for Ralph,
who drowns him out with his own reminiscences*

STAFFORD It's to do with more than that, you see. It's the
whole repressive attitude of the entire organization wherein
they are preconditioned into thinking along establishment
lines that have been laid down by a bourgeois management
class who has never had contact or serious regard for the
working artiste. It's a corporation run by mindless white-
collar morons peddling the lowest common denominator to
the highest possible audience figure with a calculated dis-
regard for the views of the programme makers or the actual
producers of creative source material whom they treat with
a total calculated cynical contempt. So that the artist's voice
is ultimately stifled.

RALPH (*over all this*) Do you know, Amy and I discovered this
spot years ago. I don't think anybody else had even heard
about it. Of course, now it's all been opened up. I'm talking
about what – thirty-eight years ago – before most of this lot
were born. Do you know, we had it practically to ourselves.
And I'll tell you something interesting. You see, up there
where that bench is now, that's where I proposed to her.
Just up there.

DORCAS Pa, I think Stafford is trying to say something.

Ralph stops speaking. So does Stafford

Sorry. I think he was saying something.

RALPH Was he? I do beg his pardon. You must excuse me.
I have a little bit of difficulty hearing on this side. Now,
what was it you were saying, old man? Sing it out.

STAFFORD (*unhappily*) I – er . . . It was just . . . I (*All the eyes upon him are too much for him. He rolls on to his back*) Oh, shit.

Ralph nods sagely and gazes at the sky, lost in his memories. Pause

RITA (*swatting*) The wasps have smelt the orange squash.
LEN (*swatting too*) Yes – yes . . .

The wasp flies to Abigail. She swats it away. It flies around for a bit, finally landing on Brenda's hair. She does not notice

MELVYN (*seeing it*) Just a sec, love.
BRENDA What?
MELVYN Nothing, keep still, it's a wasp. I'll just . . .

Melvyn goes to knock the insect from Brenda's hair, but before he can do so, she leaps into demented action
BRENDA Waah – waaah – ooh – waah – eeeeee – woooh . . .

Brenda is on her feet, dancing among the picnickers. The wasp follows her as wasps tend to do. An elaborate dance follows as other people come to their feet, either to avoid being trampled by Brenda or to protect their food from being ground underfoot or to catch the wasp or, as in Patrick's case, because she has kicked a drink over him

DORCAS (*during the above*) Don't dance about. You'll only get it angry. Sit down, you silly girl.

LEN	A wasp will never sting you unless it's provoked. It's a popular fallacy, you know, that wasps sting for no reason . . .'
RITA	Keep it away from me, keep it away from me. Keep it away.
ABIGAIL	If she'd only sit down, it'd go away. It's only after the orange squash . . .
SIMON	Keep still, why don't you keep still? If you'll all keep still, I'll catch it.
MELVYN	Don't be so daft, it's only a wasp. What are you panicking about?
PATRICK	God help us, that's all we need. An hysterical female with St Vitus's Dance.

Stafford sits huddled and isolated on the rug, unaffected by the chaos – or relatively so. Ralph views the proceedings benignly, waving his hat idly as if conducting a country dance

RALPH   (*conversationally, during the above*) Such a lot of fuss over a little insect. Good lord, what a lot of fuss.

DORCAS   (*finally topping it all*) It's all right. It's all right. Simon's got it. He's got it. Panic over. Simon's killed it.

RITA   Oh, he's killed it.

LEN   He's killed it.

They all settle down

MELVYN   What did you kill it with?

SIMON   Just with my hands. It's a trick. I learnt it in Africa, actually. Depends how fast you clap, you see. You do it like that, you see – (*he demonstrates*) – and you don't notice you've um . . . (*Examining his hand*) You don't – um . . .

ABIGAIL   You all right?

SIMON   Yes, fine.

DORCAS   Let me see.

SIMON   No, I'm all right. It usually works . . . (*He sits, staring at his palm*)

RALPH   Well done, that man.

PATRICK   I bet you put the fear of God into ants.

SIMON   Yes. And I have been known, very occasionally, to do it to human beings as well.

PATRICK   How do you mean? You clap your hands at them, do you?

SIMON   Mind you, they have to keep asking for it.

PATRICK   What? Yes, please. That sort of thing?

SIMON   Like you're doing now.

ABIGAIL   Simon, please don't.

SIMON   Because I don't mind saying, for the past half-hour, to put it bluntly, you have been getting right up my nose.

ABIGAIL   Will you please stop it.

RALPH   Hallo, hallo.

PATRICK   Well, isn't that altogether just too unfortunate?

DORCAS   Patrick.

SIMON   Yes, isn't it?

PATRICK   To coin a phrase, I think you're going to have to sniff and bear it, old boy.

SIMON   (*rising*) Is that right?

PATRICK   (*rising*) Right on, old African bush-whacker.

Abigail starts crying

DORCAS   Now chaps, fellas . . . Please. Don't start, please. She's not that worth it, believe me.

ABIGAIL   (*sharply*) What did you say?

RALPH   I think there's going to be a fight.

The rain comes down suddenly

RITA   Oh, here's the rain.

RALPH   Told you so. Didn't I tell you?

BRENDA   Oooh.

MELVYN   (*to Brenda, handing her some stuff*) Take that and run. I'll bring the rug.

In a matter of seconds, the stage empties as they flee the sudden, very violent downpour. Ralph runs with his chair over his head as an improvised umbrella. Len grabs one bag, his stool and Rita's chair. Rita clutches another bag. On her way out, assisted by Len, she falls over. Abigail, who is gathering things up, gives Len a hand to drag the limping Rita out. Patrick gathers up one or two things but disappears very swiftly to the car

The rain is very loud and the voices are barely audible

Stafford plunges out, enveloped in one of the rugs

Dorcas remains to gather things up, looking angrily after Stafford for not staying to help

Brenda runs out with the kite and personal bits

Melvyn stays to help Dorcas gather up the rest

52

Simon goes off the other way for the bicycles. Melvyn and Dorcas are the last to leave the scene. As they hurry off, they pass Abigail, now very wet, returning having helped Rita to the car

Abigail stands, alone, looking for Simon

Simon returns wheeling two bicycles. One is Abigail's old machine, and the other a newer racing version of his own. He and both machines are also very wet

ABIGAIL (*yelling above the rain*) We can't cycle in this.

SIMON What?

ABIGAIL I said, we can't cycle in this.

SIMON Well, come under the tree there. We'll soon dry out.

ABIGAIL (*unconvinced and miserably undecided*) Oh God . . . (*For a second, she stands uncommitted, getting wetter*)

SIMON Come on.

Patrick enters from the car, dry under an umbrella

PATRICK I say, can I give you a lift anywhere?

Abigail looks from one to the other. She decides

When Abigail has gone one way or the other, with one man or the other, Dorcas emerges, now also very wet, to check the picnic site for forgotten items. She happily accepts either the offer of a dry umbrella or the prospect of a wet bicycle ride. They go out

The Lights fade to a Blackout

Should Abigail have chosen to stay with Simon, Act II Scene 1 Abigail is now played. If, however, Abigail opts instead to go with Patrick, Act II Scene 1 Dorcas is played instead

Act One

Scene 2 Dorcas

The same. A bright, sunny Sunday afternoon in June

Abigail strolls on. It is apparent she is restless and discontent. She stands in the centre of the meadow and looks about her. Unseen by her, Stafford appears at the top of the slope. He is unkempt and crumpled. Half crouching with his back to her, he is evidently tracking someone or something invisible to us over the brow of the hill. He becomes aware of Abigail's presence. He stares at her, Ben Gunn-like. Abigail herself has a feeling she is being watched

ABIGAIL   (*turning and seeing him*) Wuh! Oh, hallo ...

Stafford scuttles away

Extraordinary.

Patrick enters, carrying two folding chairs, the Sunday papers and a picnic bag. He evidently considers this rather a lot to be carrying

PATRICK   (*surveying Abigail*) I take it this is your day for not carrying things? Is that correct? Yes, I thought it was. So long as we know. Never mind, the others can carry the rest. (*He dumps the stuff down and starts to put up a chair*) I really must order a special year planner just for you, you know. I mean, I know women's metabolisms go round and round in cycles but you're the only one I know who has cycles within cycles. Today is your day for not carrying things. Yesterday was your refusing-to-shut-any-doors day. Monday, if I'm not mistaken, was the yearly anniversary for the start of your leaving-all-the-taps-running week. I mean, I don't mind as long as I know they're coming. But it is nice to mark these celebrations, don't you agree? Otherwise we'll miss them. Like the International Open Fridge Door Over-

night Festival or the All British Leaving the Oven on Low
Week or the Jubilee Celebration for . . .

ABIGAIL   Oh, do shut up Patrick, for heaven's sake.

PATRICK   Right. (*Under his breath*) World Silence Day.

Patrick sits. A silence

ABIGAIL   I've done all those sandwiches. Took me all morning.
I hope Rita's remembered to do her half, that's all. Otherwise we won't have enough. She should remember. I've
phoned her enough times. I stink of sardines. God, the
organization for one simple picnic. I don't know why Pa
insists on having one. They're always disaster.

PATRICK   It won't bother me. At four-ten precisely I must be
on the motorway, steaming towards Manchester.

ABIGAIL   It's all right for you . . .

PATRICK   It isn't all right for me. I didn't arrange this
meeting. But since we have to charge round the country, we
plain simple executives, in order to humour our Chairman's
holiday arrangements . . .

ABIGAIL   Yes, I'm sure. Well, you're seeing this picnic out to
the bitter end.

PATRICK   Only until four-oh-six.

ABIGAIL   We'll see about that. You know, I thought I saw that
Stafford man just now.

PATRICK   Stafford?

ABIGAIL   You know, that peculiar poet man. The one Dorcas
used to go around with before she met up with her big game
hunter.

PATRICK   Oh, really?

ABIGAIL   I wonder what he was doing. Stafford.

PATRICK   Composing poetry? Or perhaps he's coming to the
picnic.

ABIGAIL   I hope not. No, she'd hardly invite both of them
. . . Odd.

PATRICK   What are those two kids doing? Is that daft brother
of yours playing with my car again?

55

ABIGAIL   I don't know. Go and see.

PATRICK   He cost me eighty quid last time when he cocked up the electric sunshine roof.

ABIGAIL   Ha ha.

PATRICK   You didn't think it was funny at the time, driving around in a raincoat for a month while they sent abroad for a part.

ABIGAIL   Did you good. The first fresh air you'd had for months.

Melvyn and Brenda enter. He carries the rest of the picnic gear, and Patrick's car keys. She carries a stunter kite, still in its box, and the kite strings separately

MELVYN   Here you are. I locked the car.

PATRICK   Give me the keys immediately. Did you manage to break anything?

MELVYN   No. (*Dead-pan*) Those electric windows always stop halfway up, don't they?

PATRICK   Keys.

Melvyn gives Patrick the car keys

ABIGAIL   Any sign of the others?

MELVYN   No, not yet. If they've gone by way of the cemetery they won't be here for a bit. Not with Len driving at four miles an hour.

ABIGAIL   The Sunday ritual. Well, let's get it over with. It's a perfect picnic day anyway. I take it Dorcas is coming with Simon, isn't she?

Patrick reads his papers

MELVYN   Yeah. Your brother's coming, isn't he?

BRENDA   Yes. He left home early. They were going to cycle here, I think.

ABIGAIL   Cycle?

BRENDA   Yes.

MELVYN   They cycle everywhere, didn't you know? He's the fittest man I've ever met.

ABIGAIL   Yes, but Dorcas cycling. I don't believe it. What's he done to her?

MELVYN   Dunno. Brought the kite.

ABIGAIL   (*not interested*) Oh yes.

MELVYN   (*taking it from Brenda*) Look, you see, it's a stunter.

PATRICK   (*still reading the papers*) Terrific. Don't fly it near me, will you?

MELVYN   O.K. Fair enough. (*Restlessly*) Well.

ABIGAIL   You've been round at Brenda's all morning, have you?

MELVYN   Yep. So.

ABIGAIL   Nothing. I just hope you're doing some studying, Mel. I mean, your exams are coming up in a few days, aren't they?

MELVYN   Yes, all right.

Dorcas and Simon appear at the top of the slope. They stop as they see the others. They seem flushed and happy

DORCAS   Hallo.

ABIGAIL   Hallo.

SIMON   Hallo.

MELVYN   Hi.

PATRICK   Good afternoon.

ABIGAIL   We hear you're being terribly healthy and cycling everywhere.

DORCAS   I can recommend it. Marvellous. You should have a go.

ABIGAIL   I think that's something I can live without.

PATRICK   Your bike's still hanging up in the garage if you want it.

ABIGAIL   It can stay there.

PATRICK   I'll oil it for you with pleasure. It'll save me a fortune in petrol bills.

SIMON   Is that the kite?

MELVYN   Yeah. Brand new. Bought it yesterday.

SIMON   Looks a good one.

57

MELVYN   Have you flown this sort?

SIMON   I have done.

MELVYN   Stunters?

SIMON   Yes.

MELVYN   Great.

DORCAS   Come on, let's fly it now then. I'm dying to see it.

MELVYN   Fine.

Suddenly, Brenda is galvanized into action

BRENDA   Yeeeow – wur – wur – wur – yow – wow – wow . . .

ABIGAIL   God, what's that about?

MELVYN   It's all right, it's all right.

BRENDA   It's a wasp, it's a wasp.

MELVYN   It's gone, it's gone, it's all right.

BRENDA   Wur – wur . . .

MELVYN   (*soothingly*) It's all right, calm down. It's gone. (*To the others*) She doesn't like wasps.

ABIGAIL   Yes.

SIMON   Are we off then?

MELVYN   Right.

Melvyn sets off up the hill with Brenda in tow. Simon gives Dorcas a quick hug and kiss

SIMON   (*as he does so*) Coming?

DORCAS   You bet.

SIMON   (*as they start to follow Melvyn*) There's a bit of breeze up there. They need a bit of wind, you see, these stunters. It's the type with twin lines, I take it?

MELVYN   Yes, right. Are they difficult to handle?

SIMON   No, not really. I mean, only if the wind's very strong and then they're all over the place. (*Starting to climb the slope*) No, I've seen experts handling five or six at once.

MELVYN   What, flying in formation?

SIMON   Right.

Simon, Melvyn and Brenda go

DORCAS   (*under the above, to Abigail*) You coming to watch?

ABIGAIL   Er – Dorc . . .

DORCAS   Yes.

Dorcas lingers behind while the others go off. Abigail moves to Dorcas in order to be a little way from Patrick. Having arranged this, she seems a little lost for words

Yes?

ABIGAIL   Well . . .

DORCAS   Yes. Pa gone to the cemetery first, has he?

ABIGAIL   Yes.

DORCAS   The regular weekly visit.

ABIGAIL   Yes.

PATRICK   Darling, this is the sort of lamp we need on that landing, you know.

ABIGAIL   Yes, just a second.

PATRICK   (*going back to his reading*) Not in this colour, of course.

ABIGAIL   If we ordered everything Patrick saw in the supplements, we wouldn't be able to get in the door. Haven't seen you for a bit.

DORCAS   No, well, I've been . . .

ABIGAIL   Busy.

DORCAS   Yes.

ABIGAIL   Lucky you.

DORCAS   Yes. Actually, yes.

ABIGAIL   (*abruptly*) Tell me, how does Pa seem to you these days? I mean, you see him less than I do so it's probably more noticeable to you. It's difficult for me to tell seeing him, what, two or three times a week. He does seem to me to be getting – well – a bit odd. Do you find that?

DORCAS   He's always rather odd.

ABIGAIL   Yes. He keeps telling me he's seen Mother.

DORCAS   Yes, he's told me that, too.

ABIGAIL   And sometimes, if you turn up unexpectedly, you can hear him talking to her in the other room.

59

DORCAS   He may be talking to himself.

ABIGAIL   No, no. The other day I heard him telling her a funny story. Roaring with laughter. Him that is. And then there's some days he refuses to wear socks and at least once a week he wants his bed moving round because of the way the earth's rotating. I mean, he can't be senile, can he, not yet? He's not old enough. He's only just seventy. (*She reflects*) That reminds me, it's his birthday soon.

DORCAS   I don't know why he gave up his practice. At least he met a lot of people.

ABIGAIL   Perhaps it's a good job he did. Otherwise he might have had all his patients shifting their beds about in their bare feet. Oh well, he's harmless at the moment. (*Slight pause*) You look wonderful.

DORCAS   I feel wonderful. (*Pause*) How are you?

ABIGAIL   Me?

DORCAS   And Patrick.

ABIGAIL   (*only half joking*) Don't talk about that, please.

DORCAS   All right.

Pause

ABIGAIL   (*plunging in*) I bet it's amazing, isn't it?

DORCAS   What?

ABIGAIL   With the big game hunter. It must be amazing. Isn't it?

DORCAS   Well. I don't know about that. Pretty good. I don't think I've been amazed though. Not yet.

ABIGAIL   You're looking marvellous.

DORCAS   Yes, you said.

ABIGAIL   It has that effect on some women. If they're getting it regularly, you know. They sparkle and shine. Everything about them suddenly sort of looks in good condition.

DORCAS   I washed my hair this morning. Maybe that's it.

ABIGAIL   Oh, you . . . You're so – you're always so detached.

DORCAS   No, I'm not.

ABIGAIL   Well, aren't you happy?

DORCAS   Yes, I said so.

ABIGAIL   Yes, but really happy?

DORCAS   Abi, I have never been so happy. This may sound silly but there are some moments of the day when I literally have to stand still and hold on to something. Because I'm feeling dizzy with happiness. (*Slight pause*) O.K.?

ABIGAIL   (*disconcerted*) Yes.

DORCAS   Does that answer your question?

ABIGAIL   Yes. It's all finished with your poet then?

DORCAS   Stafford? Yes, that's finished.

ABIGAIL   Did he ever write any poetry? Or did he just call himself a poet for something to put on his passport?

DORCAS   No, he wrote poetry. Not a lot. He burnt most of it in fits of fury. But some of his stuff was bloody good.

ABIGAIL   I only asked because I saw him just now, I think.

DORCAS   (*alarmed*) Stafford?

ABIGAIL   Yes, skulking. Up there. (*She indicates the slope*) He ran off as soon as he saw me.

DORCAS   (*upset*) Damn. Damn it!

ABIGAIL   Why?

DORCAS   He's still following us. How did he know we were here? I thought he'd gone home to Leicester. Oh, damn. If Simon sees him again, he'll kill him. He's been driving us mad for weeks. How did he find out we were here?

ABIGAIL   Does he follow you everywhere?

DORCAS   Yes. He has done for months. He keeps – popping up. He was in the garden the other night. I was just drawing the curtains and there he was, crouching in the flower bed. Oh, damn him, why won't he go home?

ABIGAIL   Well, perhaps he has. Perhaps he's gone now.

DORCAS   No, he hasn't. I know him. He'll be around here somewhere. (*She scans the horizon*)

PATRICK   (*still engrossed*) What's your opinion of this bath, darling? Do you think it would look any good in the guest bathroom? (*He holds up the magazine*)

ABIGAIL   Super, yes.

PATRICK   No, I'd have a closer look before you say that. It costs two thousand quid without the taps.

ABIGAIL   (*ignoring this and returning to Dorcas*) Do you know, I was just thinking, it was really only luck, wasn't it? I mean, that day. It could just as easily have been me and Simon. And if it had been the other way round, I wouldn't – I wouldn't have hesitated. Not for a second. Isn't that terrible?

Brenda enters down the slope

BRENDA   It's flying, it's flying. Look.

ABIGAIL   Oh yes.

DORCAS   Terrific.

BRENDA   (*going to her handbag, as she passes Patrick*) It's so pretty. Look, look.

PATRICK   Staggering.

BRENDA   (*moving off again*) It's really lovely. Simon, can I have a go? Please, please.

Brenda runs off

ABIGAIL   Now there's a more urgent problem.

DORCAS   What?

ABIGAIL   That. (*She nods in Brenda's direction*)

DORCAS   Oh, that. Gneeer.

ABIGAIL   I mean, dear brother's more infatuated than ever. And she gets more horrific each day. Well, I've done my bit. He won't listen to me. I've tried.

DORCAS   I think it's a lost cause.

ABIGAIL   She'll trap him into marriage eventually. She's the type. Poor kid. I mean, he knows nothing. She'll destroy the boy. We can't let that happen, can we? Gneer.

DORCAS   Gneer.

Simon and Brenda come on. Brenda holds the two control lines to an invisible kite somewhere off. She grips the plastic handles tied to the lines. Simon, behind her, attempts to guide her actions by guiding her wrists

62

SIMON   Now, keep it steady. Keep it steady. Now, pull on your left. Pull on your left. Left, left, left.

BRENDA   (*very excited*) I am, I am.

SIMON   This is your left. This one. Pull.

BRENDA   I'm pulling.

SIMON   Look out, it's going to hit the tree. Let me take it, let me take it.

MELVYN   (*off*) It's going to hit the tree.

BRENDA   It's terribly difficult.

SIMON   That's it, I've got it, I've got it. There she goes.

MELVYN   (*off, distant*) Well done.

DORCAS   Hey, isn't that great? Look at it? He's brilliant.

SIMON   There she goes.

DORCAS   I want a turn, please. I want a turn.

SIMON   Sure. Come here. Take over.

DORCAS   Is it difficult?

SIMON   No, not at all.

BRENDA   (*running off to rejoin Melvyn*) Don't believe him. It's terribly difficult.

Brenda goes

SIMON   (*enveloping Dorcas between his arms to allow a take-over of the controls*) Now, here. Take the lines. That's it, one in each hand. Now, you pull that and it goes that way. And that makes it go that way. With a bit of practice, you can do that.

DORCAS   Hey!

SIMON   That's it. Let it come back.

DORCAS   Tremendous.

SIMON   Otherwise you'll lose the wind. It's too sheltered down here, you see.

DORCAS   Hey! Look, Abi, isn't this sensational?

ABIGAIL   Yes.

Brenda screams, off

DORCAS   Whey . . .

MELVYN   (*off, distant*) Careful.

DORCAS Sorry. Mind your nut.

Dorcas moves off, controlling the kite

Simon watches with a protective eye. Abigail studies Simon. Patrick reads on

PATRICK No, I'm sorry, I was wrong. It's two thousand quid but they do throw in the taps. That's better. I was going to say . . .

ABIGAIL Oh well, let's have three then . . .

SIMON You going to have a go later?

ABIGAIL No. I don't think so. It looks a bit complicated.

SIMON There's nothing to it. Just a knack. Once you've got the hang of it, you're . . .

Dorcas laughs, off

(*Watching the kite's manœuvres*) Hey. (*To Abigail*) How are you keeping, then? Haven't seen you for a bit.

ABIGAIL (*shrugging*) Oh – you know.

Dorcas laughs, off

SIMON She's really getting the hang of that. (*Calling*) Well done.

DORCAS (*off*) Thanks.

ABIGAIL That's Dorcas. Anything in that line.

SIMON It's good to see her relaxing. I mean, it's marvellous this job she's got and these programmes she does are really first rate. Have you heard any of them?

ABIGAIL No. Of course we can't really get it very well where we are – local radio. We're on the edge of the area. Or in a dip or something.

SIMON It really is first class. But they do expect them to work awfully hard on these local radio stations. I mean, she has to get up at dawn twice a week to read the farming news.

ABIGAIL That must be a bit disruptive for you.

SIMON   Still, it gives us an excuse for an early night, I suppose
(*He laughs*)

ABIGAIL   (*somewhat cool*) Yes.

SIMON   (*immediately embarrassed*) Oh well, holidays are over soon.
I start teaching again this autumn. Of course, I used to
teach before I went abroad. P.E. and games, you know.

ABIGAIL   Is that what you did in Africa?

SIMON   No, no. I was with this firm. Machine tools.

ABIGAIL   Ah.

SIMON   Then they got taken over and nationalized and I was
made redundant.

ABIGAIL   How terrible. They were sending all the Europeans
packing, were they?

SIMON   No, not as far as I know. Just me. Most of the chaps
seemed to be lucky.

ABIGAIL   Ah.

SIMON   Still. No regrets.

ABIGAIL   It must have been exciting, though. Africa.

SIMON   Well, different. Yes, it's an exciting place.

ABIGAIL   Makes me feel restless. There's this awful civilizing
domesticating streak in us, isn't there? Urging us to curb our
natural adventurous selves. To settle for the second best.

SIMON   Don't let your husband hear you say that.

ABIGAIL   I meant within ourselves, actually.

SIMON   Oh yes. Sorry.

ABIGAIL   Though, possibly ... I don't know. I do know
there's a lot more in me than I'm allowed to express.

SIMON   Well, that's true of most of us, I think.

Dorcas screams, off

(*Calling*) Mind the trees.

ABIGAIL   Not all of us. The lucky ones – take Dorcas, for
instance – I mean, there she is totally fulfilled. She's at full
stretch, doing what she wants to do. The Dorcas you see
there is the total Dorcas. That's her. No more, no less. I
mean, emotionally speaking. What you see is what you get.

65

Dorcas bounds into view still holding on to the kite

DORCAS (*over her shoulder*) Were you watching?

SIMON Yes.

ABIGAIL Very good.

DORCAS It's great fun.

SIMON (*drawing further away from Dorcas*) I mean, when you say that, you're not implying she's shallow, are you? Because I can't agree with that.

ABIGAIL Good lord, no.

DORCAS What are you two doing?

SIMON Watching you. (*Returning to Abigail*) I still think, though, that what you're saying about her could be said about most of us.

ABIGAIL Not everyone. I'm the reverse, I'm afraid. An incurable idealist.

SIMON Aha.

ABIGAIL If I could live in the clouds all day – like that thing . . . (*She indicates the kite*)

BRENDA (*off*) Ooh!

DORCAS (*momentarily losing control; to Melvyn and Brenda off*) Whoops, sorry, look out!

ABIGAIL Well, perhaps not quite like that thing . . . But you know what I mean.

SIMON A dreamer, eh?

ABIGAIL How does it go now:

'The desire of the moth for the star
Of the night for the morrow
The devotion to something afar
From the sphere of our sorrow?'
That's it, isn't it?

SIMON (*unsure*) Yes, yes.

ABIGAIL Who is that now? Byron . . .

SIMON That's it, that's it.

ABIGAIL No, Shelley. Of course it's Shelley.

SIMON Shelley, yes. Sorry. I'm not too hot on Shelley.

ABIGAIL I mean, I know, I just know that given the chance
there's so much I could give, that's just at present being
wasted.

SIMON Yes, I know what you mean.

DORCAS (*still struggling with the kite but trying to get a better look*)
Does someone else want a go now?

ABIGAIL I mean, it's not that I blame – (*nodding in Patrick's
direction*) – over there. Well, not entirely. But I know in the
right circumstances – in the right hands, if you want to put
it like that – I could – and of course it would be the same
for him – God knows what I could. It would be a total
commitment. The sort of thing I suppose that most of us
draw back from instinctively.

SIMON Yes, well, I mean if you really are talking about total
. . .

ABIGAIL Yes, I am.

DORCAS All right, I'm going to land it now. Mind your heads.

SIMON I mean, let's just define what we're talking about. Are
we talking spiritually or emotionally or physically . . .

ABIGAIL Well, I would have hoped all three. Wouldn't you?

SIMON Right, right.

ABIGAIL My God, when I – if I give myself, and note the
word 'self', as far as I'm concerned that means all of me.
(*Indicating her body*) All this, to put it absolutely crudely.

SIMON Good, good.

ABIGAIL I mean, the only condition that I would ever lay
down is that the other person comes prepared to take. And
not sit reading the bloody Sunday papers all day, if you'll
pardon the language.

DORCAS (*still at the controls*) Whoo! Down she comes.

ABIGAIL Still, that's my problem.

SIMON (*laughing*) Yes. Well . . .

ABIGAIL Believe me, boy, you've made the right choice.
Between us two.

SIMON Oh, well . . .

ABIGAIL I'm afraid I seem to have got the reputation as the one who chews men up for breakfast and then spits them out in small pieces. I think it's still considered rather unbecoming for women to have large appetites. In some quarters that is.

SIMON   Depends which quarters.

ABIGAIL   Wing three quarters, perhaps?

SIMON   Well, that's all right, I'm in the scrum.

ABIGAIL   (*laughing gaily*) Oh, that's very funny.

DORCAS   (*landing the kite*) Touch down. There. (*She slides down the bank to join them*)

ABIGAIL   (*through the above*) That's very, very funny.

DORCAS   I have just given it a perfect one-point landing.

SIMON   Well done.

DORCAS   Don't ask me to try and get it up again. I can bring it down but I can't get it up again.

ABIGAIL   That's your problem, dear.

DORCAS   Don't be disgusting, Abigail. You'll have to excuse my sister, Simon. She has a depraved mind.

SIMON   Ah.

DORCAS   I am the only pure one in this family.

Melvyn appears on the brow of the hill

MELVYN   That was a good landing. Are we taking it up again?

Brenda appears beside Melvyn

SIMON   Yes, if you like.

BRENDA   (*examining her bare foot*) I've got a splinter.

SIMON   (*going up the bank*) You stand by to launch it. I'll take the controls.

MELVYN   Right.

ABIGAIL   (*following*) You know, I think I'm going to have a go at this, it does look fun.

DORCAS   It's very hard work. You won't like that.

Abigail pulls a face at Dorcas and goes on up the hill to where Melvyn, Brenda and Simon are. Melvyn gathers up the control lines where Dorcas has laid them down

MELVYN   We'd better go back this way a bit.

ABIGAIL   Remember I'm having the next go.

Abigail and Melvyn go off

SIMON   (*turning back to Dorcas and blowing her a kiss*) All right, darling?

DORCAS   Yes, be with you in a minute.

SIMON   O.K. (*To Brenda, who is still examining the bottom of her foot*) Come along then, Hopalong.

BRENDA   I've got an awful splinter.

Simon and Brenda go off

Dorcas and Patrick are silent for a second

PATRICK   I thought kites were supposed to be quiet things. Do you want something to read?

DORCAS   No, thanks.

PATRICK   (*holding out the magazine*) What do you think of this bath?

DORCAS   (*moving closer*) Where?

PATRICK   This bath, there. What's your opinion?

DORCAS   I think it's absolutely foul.

PATRICK   Oh, do you?

DORCAS   Awful.

PATRICK   Oh. I was just coming round to liking it . . . You're probably right.

Simon appears over the brow of the hill. He holds a limp, unresisting Stafford by his collar. Stafford hangs from Simon's grip like an old suit in need of dry-cleaning

SIMON   Look what I've found, snivelling in the bushes.

DORCAS   Oh, Stafford. What are you doing here?

SIMON   I caught him tinkering with the bikes. He was on the point of letting my tyres down.

DORCAS   How did you know we were here? Who told you?

Stafford does not reply

69

SIMON   (*rattling him slightly*) Who told you?

DORCAS   Oh, Simon, don't do that to him . . .

SIMON   I'll do a damn sight more to him than this in a minute.

DORCAS   Simon!

SIMON   I'm sorry, Dorc, I'm absolutely sick to the back teeth with this little gobbit crawling around after us.

DORCAS   Well, don't do that to him, please. He's got a weak chest. If you shake him about like that, he'll cough for hours.

SIMON   Oh, damn it. (*He drops Stafford in a heap*)

DORCAS   Now, Stafford, what do you think you're playing at? (*Silence*) Stafford? (*Silence*) Simon, would you mind?

SIMON   What?

DORCAS   Leave us for a second.

SIMON   (*reluctantly*) O.K. (*To Stafford, menacingly*) You just watch yourself, Sunbeam.

Simon goes up the hill

DORCAS   (*when they are alone*) Staff, now listen . . .

Stafford looks at Patrick

It's all right, he can't hear us. (*To Patrick*) Can you?

PATRICK   What?

DORCAS   I'm saying you can't hear us, can you?

PATRICK   I beg your pardon?

DORCAS   Oh, shut up. Stafford, what are you doing? You will simply have to go home. Look, you can't keep creeping about in our garden at all hours. And it was you who has been sleeping in our shed, wasn't it? (*No reply*) It's over, Staff. Go home. Go home and please – have a bath.

STAFFORD   I love you.

DORCAS   (*ignoring this*) Do you need money?

STAFFORD   (*doggedly*) I love you.

DORCAS   Sssh. Have you got money for your train fare?

STAFFORD   Did you hear me? I love you.

DORCAS   (*as kindly as she can*) Yes, but I don't love you, Stafford. I'm sorry but that's the truth. You'll have to face that.

I don't love you. It isn't entirely my fault and I don't know why I should be feeling guilty about it. I mean, I've tried my best to help you, Stafford. I even employed you on my programme. And what do you do? You start a fight in the B.B.C. canteen. That vision mixer is still off work, Stafford. And none of the Sports Unit will talk to me at all. It isn't true either that I gave you the job out of pity. I admire you. I do, I admire your poetry, I – well, you know what I think of your politics but I've always admired your seriousness over them. I wish I could be that serious. And most of all, I wish I was still in love with you but I'm not. I can't help it. I love Simon. I'm sorry.

STAFFORD   (*calmly*) I'm going to kill him.

DORCAS   Stafford, please. I'm sorry.

STAFFORD   (*shaking his head*) Then what's the point? (*He stands; louder*) What's the point? (*Screaming as he runs off*) What's the bloody point of it all?

DORCAS   (*vainly, after him*) Stafford . . .!

Stafford goes

PATRICK   (*wincing at this added interruption*) Oh my God.

Simon is over the hill in a flash

SIMON   You all right?

DORCAS   Yes.

SIMON   Sure?

DORCAS   I hope he's not going to do anything stupid.

SIMON   It's O.K., I'll keep an eye on him. If he steps out of line, I'll kill him. Simple as that.

DORCAS   Oh dear. I'd love to know who told him we were here.

SIMON   I don't know. Who could've done?

Abigail appears breathless at the top of the hill

DORCAS   (*in Abigail's direction*) I don't know.

ABIGAIL   (*regaining her breath*) They're here. We've just spotted the car.

71

Melvyn appears over the hill holding the kite. Brenda follows on, still limping. She is finishing re-winding one of the kite strings back on to its handle

(*Meanwhile, coming down the slope*) I hope Rita remembered to bring the other sandwiches. (*To Patrick*) Do try and enjoy yourself, won't you darling?

PATRICK   (*rising to knot his tie*) Don't worry about me. I'll have a whale of a time. I'm about to leave in forty-five seconds.

ABIGAIL   Oh no, you're not, you know.

PATRICK   (*unfussed*) Oh yes, I am, you know.

ABIGAIL   (*to Dorcas, hardly heeding this last, with chair*) Was that Stafford rushing about just now?

DORCAS   Yes.

ABIGAIL   He nearly strangled himself in kite string. I hope he's not going to be trouble.

DORCAS   He won't.

Ralph comes on

ABIGAIL   Hallo, Pa.

RALPH   At last, at last, Sorry we're late.

ABIGAIL   You're not late.

RALPH   Hallo there, Patrick. Nice to see you.

PATRICK   (*shaking him by the hand*) Hallo there, Ralph, cheerio. Sorry I couldn't stay longer. I hope you have a really nice picnic.

ABIGAIL   (*hissing*) Patrick.

PATRICK   Got the weather for it, anyway.

RALPH   Oh, you're off, are you?

PATRICK   'Fraid so. Manchester calls.

ABIGAIL   Patrick.

RALPH   Oh well, good luck. Cheerio then.

ABIGAIL   (*sweetly*) Patrick, you cannot leave now.

PATRICK   (*returning to kiss her*) Oh my darling, of course. (*In her ear*) I told you.

ABIGAIL   (*in his ear*) You bastard.

PATRICK 'Bye 'bye all. Darling, have a look at that bath when you've a minute. See what you think.

ABIGAIL Yes, of course. (*Sweetly*) As long as it's deep enough to get your head under.

PATRICK 'Bye 'bye.

Patrick goes

ALL (*variously*) 'Bye.

DORCAS (*holding one of the chairs*) Where do you want to sit, Father?

RALPH Just where you are, my dearest, as long as it's out of the wind. Mel, boy, see if your Uncle Len needs a hand, will you?

Melvyn comes down the slope. Brenda limps after him

And there's your girl. How's she? Good lord, she looks as if she's gone lame. You'll have to put her down, Mel.

BRENDA I've got a splinter.

Melvyn goes off

RALPH Good girl, good girl. (*To Simon*) Going to be a fine doctor one day, that boy, if he ever gets his exams. Ah now, and how are you – er – young – er . . .

SIMON Simon.

RALPH Simon. Excellent. Did Dorcas bring you?

SIMON Yes.

RALPH Splendid. I saw your other fellow this morning, Dorcas. The poet one. You know the chap. Strathclyde? No . . .

DORCAS Stafford

RALPH Stafford, that's the one. I was in the potting shed and I fell over him. I don't know what he was doing. So I asked him to the picnic. But he didn't seem very interested. Ran off shouting something. Very odd bloke, isn't he?

DORCAS Yes, Father.

SIMON (*coldly furious*) Right, that's his lot.

73

RALPH Bit of in-breeding there, I wouldn't be surprised.

SIMON Next time I see him, that's it.

DORCAS (*moving to Simon, still holding the chair*) Simon . . .

RALPH (*to Dorcas with the chair*) No, not there, old lumpkin. A bit further round. I don't want it blowing down my neck, do I?

Melvyn enters with a fishing stool and a rug

(*Sitting*) That's better, that's better. Splendid. Thank you, Mel. Is Len managing?

MELVYN Yeah. He's padlocking up the hubcaps.

RALPH I was telling them, Mel. If you keep your nose in your books and don't spend every second of every day ogling what's'ername there, you'll be a very fine doctor.

MELVYN (*spreading out the rug for him and Brenda, unmoved*) Yeah.

RALPH (*without offence*) He doesn't listen to a blasted word I say, does he? Well, this is nice, isn't it? We'd better get our tea in before the rain, that's all.

DORCAS What rain?

RALPH Look over there. See those clouds? Well, twenty minutes they'll be overhead.

ABIGAIL Nonsense.

RALPH Betcha. Seen it before.

SIMON (*to Dorcas*) Why's he only got one sock on?

DORCAS God knows.

Rita comes on with more bags

RITA Here we are. I see Patrick's off already.

ABIGAIL Yes. Never mind, we'll survive.

RALPH Over here, Rita. We've reserved you a spot over here.

RITA We've been locking the car.

Len enters with other picnickery

LEN Can't be too careful. Not these days.

RALPH Won't do to have a copper having his car nicked, will it?

74

LEN If I related to you the statistics regarding car thefts for one month in this area, it would horrify you. Horrify you. We don't release the true figures. The general public would panic.

RALPH Yes, yes.

DORCAS Hope my bike's all right.

LEN Locked it up, have you?

DORCAS No, it's just under a bush over there.

LEN It is quite within bounds that by the time you get back to it, they'll have stripped it of everything.

RITA Stripped it.

LEN Bell, gears, lights back and front, wheels, rear reflectors, both sets of brakes and the saddle.

RITA Rear reflectors.

LEN And if it's a lady's bike and you're out of luck, they'll be lying in wait to rape you as well.

DORCAS Oh, thanks a million, Uncle Len.

LEN Just a warning. (*He sits on the stool*)

SIMON (*grimly*) Don't worry. Anyone comes within a yard of those bikes . . .

RALPH There you are, she's got a watchdog. She's all right. (*To Dorcas*) You're all right.

DORCAS (*strained*) Yes.

ABIGAIL Now Rita, you have remembered to bring your sandwiches?

RITA (*tapping her basket*) Yes, they're in here. Did you bring yours?

ABIGAIL Yes, they're there.

RALPH Well, that's all right for you two. What are the rest of us going to eat?

ABIGAIL No, Pa. Rita and I have done half each, that's all.

RALPH That's all right. As long as you washed your hands first, Abi. This girl, she'd never wash her hands, you know. We used to have to hold her under a tap. She was the grubby one, this one.

ABIGAIL All right, Pa.

RALPH (*to Brenda*) Have you got that thing out of your foot yet?

BRENDA No.

RALPH Well, put your hoof in your mouth and suck it. Can you suck your foot?

BRENDA No.

RALPH Dear oh dear. (*To Len*) She can't be much fun, can she?

DORCAS He's going completely mad.

RALPH Come on, then. Let's eat before the rain.

DORCAS It's not going to rain.

RALPH Wait and see. Wait and see.

RITA Are you all right on that stool, Len?

LEN Oh yes. Many an hour I've spent on this stool watching the rod.

RITA (*sorting out the bags*) Now then.

RALPH Still fish, do you, Len?

LEN Not as much as I did. Not as much as I'd like to.

RITA He's no time, have you?

LEN Not any more.

RITA Now what have we got in here?

ABIGAIL All right, nobody move. Rita and I will do it.

DORCAS No, Abi, let me help.

ABIGAIL No, Dorc. Just sit down. Everyone sit down.

DORCAS Abi, please.

ABIGAIL Sit down. Do as you're told.

RALPH I don't know why you don't leave it to Dorcas, Abi. We always do that in this family, Simon. When it comes to organization we leave it to Dorcas.

SIMON Ah.

ABIGAIL Well, she's not the only one who can organize, so there.

Rita unpacks the first batch of sandwiches from her own bag: eight cheese and tomato. All sandwiches referred to are half rounds

RITA Here we are.

ABIGAIL   Splendid. Now then, what are these?

RITA   Cheese and tomato, those are.

RALPH   Splendid.

ABIGAIL   (*handing Simon a stack of eight paper plates*) Simon, could you hand these out, please?

SIMON   Certainly.

Simon gives himself and Dorcas a plate, then pauses

ABIGAIL   (*taking the sandwiches from Rita*) Now . . . Hang on a tick, are these the ones I made?

RITA   No, those are the ones I made.

ABIGAIL   Cheese and tomato?

RITA   Yes.

ABIGAIL   You were supposed to be making egg and tomato.

RITA   No, cheese and tomato.

ABIGAIL   No, Rita. We have had phone call after phone call about this. You were supposed to be making egg and tomato. I was supposed to be making cheese and tomato. I have now made cheese and tomato.

RITA   Well, I've made cheese and tomato as well.

ABIGAIL   Oh, godfathers.

MELVYN   Hands up anyone who doesn't like cheese and tomato.

ABIGAIL   Be quiet. What else have you made, don't tell me . . .

RITA   Sardine and . . .

ABIGAIL   Sardine and cucumber . . .

RITA   Cucumber – yes.

ABIGAIL   Oh dear heaven.

Simon serves Len and Rita

RALPH   Len. Who does she remind you of now? Abigail? Who is it she's like now?

ABIGAIL   I apologize everyone. I'm afraid you have the grand choice of either cheese and tomato or sardine and cucumber.

77

LEN Amy? Just like her mother.

RALPH Amy, that's right.

ABIGAIL And there are a great deal of those so I hope you like them.

RALPH Once she's roused, you know, she's all Amy. Like a duchess.

Simon serves Ralph

ABIGAIL Father darling, please put a sock in it. Or rather . . .

DORCAS (*springing up*) Cheese and tomato everyone.

ABIGAIL No, I'll do them.

Simon gives Brenda and Melvyn plates

Abigail takes round the sandwiches, serving first Len, then her own plate, then Dorcas and finally Simon's plate where she stops

RALPH (*to Len, as Abigail hands round the sandwiches*) Abi's like me. We're the fly-by-nights. Hopping about from this to that. (*To Abigail*) Aren't you?

ABIGAIL (*putting a sandwich on to Simon's plate*) Nonsense. (*Suddenly, in a low voice to Dorcas*) God.

DORCAS (*in a low voice*) What?

ABIGAIL Don't look now, he's over there. In the bushes. Stafford. He's in the bushes.

DORCAS (*rising*) Where?

ABIGAIL Don't stare. In the bushes.

Dorcas takes the plate of sandwiches from Abigail as a pretext for looking at Stafford unobserved. She puts a sandwich on to Simon's plate

DORCAS God, if Simon sees him . . .

ABIGAIL (*moving away*) Keep going, keep going.

Dorcas, keeping one eye on the bushes and Stafford who is at present out of view to us, having served Simon's plate retraces Abigail's steps, serving her own, then Abigail and finally Len. Abigail meantime returns for the next batch of sandwiches, which are Rita's sardine and cucumber. Abigail in a moment hands these to Simon. She then concentrates on unpacking the paper cups and two thermos flasks, one of which contains tea, the other orange squash. Len, at this point, goes to check his car, without going off

MELVYN (*catching sight of Stafford*) Hey, look who I can see. Over . . .

ABIGAIL (*drowning him*) You going to fly your kite after tea, Mel? (*She indicates Simon*)

MELVYN Oh. (*Realizing*) Yes.

DORCAS You all right, Uncle Len?

LEN (*returning*) Just checking the car.

SIMON (*to Melvyn, puzzled*) Who can you see where?

ABIGAIL (*thrusting the sardine and cucumber at Simon*) Simon, could you serve these?

SIMON Right.

Simon starts to serve sardine and cucumber: first to Rita, then to Ralph, then Brenda and finally Melvyn. At this point, he is interrupted

DORCAS (*moving close to Abigail*) I think he's gone.

ABIGAIL Thank God.

LEN (*to Simon*) Rumour has it, you're an athlete, young man.

SIMON (*as he serves*) Well, used to be.

LEN Were you a runner, by any chance?

RALPH Careful how you answer that question, Simon.

SIMON Well, yes, I used to run a bit.

Abigail, rising with cups, now catches sight of Stafford somewhere behind Melvyn

ABIGAIL (*to Dorcas*) My God, he's over there now. Look.

Dorcas looks

DORCAS Where?

ABIGAIL There.

SIMON I'm certainly not a sprinter.

79

LEN Cross-country at all?

Dorcas intercepts Simon as he reaches Melvyn and is liable to catch sight of Stafford

DORCAS (*taking the sardine and cucumber from Simon*) Let me do those, Si. Can you do the cups?

SIMON Sure. (*To Len*) Cross-country? Well, a bit. Not recently.

RALPH Ah-ha. Ah-ha.

Dorcas, with one eye out for Stafford, retraces Simon's steps, serving Melvyn, then Brenda, Ralph and finally Rita

RITA Here we are.

Rita hands Abigail the second box of cheese and tomato made by Abigail. Abigail then serves first Len, then her own plate and finally Dorcas and Simon's plate. Meanwhile Simon goes round with the cups, starting with his own

SIMON Why are you asking? Were you a runner?

LEN Years ago. Years ago.

RALPH He was very good.

RITA He ran for the Police.

Abigail has sighted Stafford in another direction

ABIGAIL Dorc . . .

DORCAS (*moving to her*) Yes?

ABIGAIL He's over there now, the little bastard.

DORCAS (*panicking slightly*) What are we going to do?

ABIGAIL Keep calm. He's gone again.

Dorcas takes the plate from Abigail and retraces Abigail's steps, serving Simon's plate, her own plate, Abigail's plate and finally Len with cheese and tomato

LEN (*during the above*) No, I organize the local cross-country derby once a year. It's a light-hearted jaunt, but we usually get quite a good field.

Abigail returns and takes from Rita the second batch of sardine and cucumber. She serves these to Rita, Ralph, Brenda and then Melvyn

RALPH   Light-hearted, he says.

LEN   We run it around here.

SIMON   Sounds fun.

LEN   I might persuade you to enter then?

MELVYN   (*as Abigail serves him*) He's over there now.

ABIGAIL   Yes.

SIMON   Well . . .

ABIGAIL   Simon, could you serve these, please?

SIMON   Right. (*To Len*) I'll see.

Simon serves Melvyn, Brenda, Ralph and finally Rita during the following

RALPH   You know, Len, I'd fancy him against Murphy, you know.

LEN   Oh no, no. Nobody beats Murphy.

SIMON   Murphy?

RALPH   Young Constable Murphy. Finest runner I've seen for some time.

RITA   Len's brought him on from nothing.

LEN   No, he won't touch Murphy. Promise you that.

DORCAS   Wha! (*She kicks a bush*)

ABIGAIL   What about drinks?

RITA   It's all right, Abi, I'll do those.

LEN   Well, it's not till September the eighth. You've plenty of time.

SIMON   I might just be fit by then, I suppose.

RITA   Now, those who don't want tea put your hands up.

Melvyn and Brenda, Simon and Dorcas all put their hands up

   (*Starting to count*) That's one, two . . .

RALPH   (*putting up his hand*) Is this for tea?

RITA   No, this is not for tea.

RALPH   Ah, this is not for tea. (*He puts his hand down*)

LEN Not for tea? (*Putting up his hand*) No, I'm for tea. One here.

RITA Then put your hand down. This is not for tea. Right. That's one, two, three, four not for tea. Now, hands up for orange squash.

The same hands go up

MELVYN It'll be the same people.

RITA What will?

MELVYN It'll be the same people who aren't for tea.

RITA Who are?

MELVYN The ones who want orange squash.

RITA If you want orange squash, put your hand up.

MELVYN It'll be the same. If you subtract the people who don't want tea from the people who are here, you'll get the people who do want tea, won't you? It's obvious the people who don't want tea must want . . .

ABIGAIL Put your hand up, Mel, and shut up.

MELVYN (*putting his hand up, muttering*) It'll be the same.

RITA I don't know what he's talking about, I'm sure. That's one, two, three, four orange squash.

MELVYN (*muttering to Brenda*) I told her it would be the same.

During the following, Rita starts to serve the drinks from the two thermos flasks. The others help ferry the cups to and fro. At the finish, Ralph, Len, Rita and Abigail have tea. Simon, Brenda, Melvyn and Dorcas have orange squash. Abigail pours one cup of tea

RALPH Anyone any the wiser after all that?

ABIGAIL You have tea, Pa. Here you are.

RALPH Ah-ha. Look, I'm sorry to cast a pall on the proceedings but it wouldn't be possible, would it, to have a spot more variety as regards sandwiches?

ABIGAIL Yes, I'm sorry, I explained. Rita and I had a mix-up.

RALPH It's just I have a sea of sardines and acres of cucumber.

ABIGAIL You should have cheese and tomato as well.

RALPH No. No cheese, no tomato.

LEN Well, I have. I've got all cheese and all tomato.

MELVYN We haven't. We've got sardine and cucumber.

DORCAS I've got cheese and tomato.

ABIGAIL Oh, dear God. Right, hands up who've got sardines and cucumber.

Ralph, Rita, Brenda, Melvyn put up their hands

Right. Now hands up who've only got cheese and tomato.

MELVYN It'll be the people who haven't . . .

ABIGAIL (*shouting loudly*) Melvyn! Cheese and tomato, please.

Dorcas, Len and Simon put up their hands

And I think it'll be me as well. (*Examining her plate*) Yes.

LEN Keep talking normally, everyone.

ABIGAIL What?

LEN I think we're being observed.

RITA What's the matter?

LEN No cause for alarm. But I think we're being watched by a prowler.

SIMON By a what? If that's who I . . .

DORCAS (*springing up*) Right. Now let's get these sandwiches sorted out. When I give the word, I want Melvyn to give two sandwiches to Len and Len to give two sandwiches to Melvyn. Simon give two sandwiches to Rita. Rita give two sandwiches to Simon. Brenda give two sandwiches to Abi. Abi give two sandwiches to Brenda. Pa, you give me two of yours and I'll give you two of mine. All right, everybody, thank you. Off we go.

Confusion as people exchange sandwiches

Meanwhile Stafford appears at the top of the bank. He slithers down and hides behind the bench

Now has everybody got what they want?

RALPH   Lovely, lovely. I told you she was good at organizing.

RITA   What was this about prowlers?

LEN   (*looking where Stafford was*) I think he's gone now.

RITA   Good.

ABIGAIL   (*leaning in to Dorcas*) He's behind the bench.

DORCAS   I know. He's getting closer.

RALPH   Well, we've beaten the rain.

RITA   Yes, they're coming closer.

RALPH   Told you so. Well, just to say thank you all for coming along and humouring me. I'm sure you've all got other things you'd far rather be doing.

ABIGAIL   No, I'm sure we haven't. Have we?

DORCAS   No.

RALPH   I must say when I told Amy on Wednesday, she was very, very touched. She wanted me to thank you.

LEN   Ah.

RITA   Oh.

DORCAS   Good.

Slight pause

RALPH   It may be my imagination but I think I can see Stratford.

LEN   Stratford?

RITA   Not from here, surely.

RALPH   Behind that bench. Lying down. Do you see?

LEN   Good grief.

DORCAS   Stafford, Father. His name's Stafford.

RALPH   Stafford. That's it. I'm always getting him wrong.

LEN   That's him. That's the prowler.

RITA   Oh.

DORCAS   It's all right, Uncle Len. I mean, you can't arrest someone for lying behind a bench, can you?

LEN   Depends what he's doing behind the bench, doesn't it?

ABIGAIL   It's all right, he's a friend.

LEN   He's known to you, is he?

84

SIMON (*finishing his sandwich with finality*) He's certainly known
   to me. (*Rising*) Excuse me.

DORCAS Simon.

RALPH Going to be a fight, is there?

SIMON Excuse me a moment.

ABIGAIL Simon . . .

DORCAS Simon, please.

SIMON Won't be one moment. (*He moves towards the bench and
   Stafford*)

RALPH He's quite harmless, this Stratford, Len. He spends
   a lot of time in our shed but he's quite harmless.

LEN (*unconvinced*) I see.

*Simon reaches the bench. Stafford lies still. Simon puts one foot up on
the bench*

SIMON (*with his back to the others, conversationally*) Listen, old
   chap, if you continue to follow Dorcas and me around for
   a moment longer, I shall personally pull off both your arms
   and stick them up your nose. And that will just be for
   starters. Now do us all an enormous favour, be a good chap
   and just bugger off.

Stafford rises, alarmed

   That's a good chap.

STAFFORD (*menacingly, retreating*) Right – right . . .

   Stafford goes

RALPH (*as the others watch*) He's got rid of him.

SIMON (*returning*) That's that.

DORCAS What did you say to him?

SIMON Just asked him to leave.

LEN You can't be too careful. This is a favourite spot, this
   is. I mean, we're all right now in broad daylight but I
   wouldn't care to be sitting up here like this in the middle
   of the night.

ABIGAIL Why?

85

LEN   Let us just say it is a favourite haunt.

RITA   Haunted?

LEN   No, not haunted. I'm saying it is a haunt for certain undesirables who wish to practise unnatural practices.

MELVYN   Unnatural practices?

LEN   I'm saying no more.

MELVYN   What unnatural practices?

LEN   I think I've said enough on that subject.

DORCAS   Well, I can promise you that has nothing to do with Stafford.

LEN   I hope not, for his sake. Because we shall catch up with them and then . . .

MELVYN   (*to Brenda*) We must come up here at night.

LEN   Now, don't be young, lad, don't be young. Be your age.

A pause

RITA   (*swatting*) The wasps have smelt the orange squash.

LEN   (*swatting too*) Yes. Yes . . .

The wasp flies to Abigail. She swats it away. It flies around for a bit, finally landing on Brenda's hair. She does not notice

MELVYN   (*seeing it*) Just a sec, love.

BRENDA   What?

MELVYN   Nothing, keep still, it's a wasp. I'll just . . .

Melvyn goes to knock the insect from Brenda's hair, but before he can do so, she leaps into demented action

BRENDA   Waaah – waaah – ooh – waah – eeeeee – woooh . . .

Brenda dances among the picnickers. The wasp follows her as wasps tend to do. An elaborate dance follows as other people come to their feet, either to avoid being trampled by Brenda or to protect their food from being ground underfoot or to catch the wasp or because she has knocked a drink over them

DORCAS   (*during the above*) Don't dance about. You'll only get it angry. Sit down, you silly girl.

LEN | A wasp will never sting you unless it's provoked. It's a popular fallacy, you know, that wasps sting for no reason . . .

RITA | Keep it away from me, keep it away from me. Keep it away.

ABIGAIL | If she'd only sit down, it'd go away. It's only after the orange squash . . .

SIMON | Keep still, why don't you keep still? If you'll all keep still, I'll catch it.

MELVYN | Don't be so daft, it's only a wasp. What are you panicking about?

Ralph views the proceedings benignly, waving his hat idly as if conducting a country dance

RALPH (*conversationally, during the above*) Such a lot of fuss over a little insect. Good lord, what a lot of fuss.

DORCAS (*finally topping it all*) It's all right. It's all right. Simon's got it. He's got it. Panic over. Simon's killed it.

RITA Oh, he's killed it.

LEN He's killed it.

They all settle down

MELVYN What did you kill it with?

SIMON Just with my hands. It's a trick. I learnt it in Africa, actually. Depends how fast you clap, you see. You do it like that, you see. (*He does so*) And you don't notice you've – um . . . (*Examining his hand*) You don't – um . . .

ABIGAIL You all right?

SIMON Yes, fine.

DORCAS Let me see.

SIMON No, I'm all right. It usually works . . . (*He stares at his palm*)

RALPH Well done, that man.

ABIGAIL Very impressive. I bet you're sensational with a charging rhino, aren't you?

SIMON   I don't know. Luckily, I never had to find out.

Stafford appears at the top of the slope astride a bicycle. He gives a blood curdling yell

The picnickers are frozen

STAFFORD   (*kicking off and plunging down the slope*) Geronimo!

There are screams as people scatter. Stafford lands in the middle of them. Simon grabs him. He comes off the bike. He and Simon grapple. Dorcas is half-shouting, half-crying. The rain comes down suddenly

RITA   Oh, here's the rain.
RALPH   Told you so. Didn't I tell you?
BRENDA   Ooh.
MELVYN   (*to her, handing her some stuff*) Take that and run. I'll bring the rug.

In a matter of seconds, the stage empties as they flee the sudden, very violent downpour. Ralph runs with his chair over his head as an improvised umbrella. Len grabs one bag, his stool and Rita's chair. Rita clutches another bag

As soon as the rain starts, Stafford darts away, escaping Simon's grip

Simon thinks of following, but decides better of it. He examines the bicycle instead

DORCAS   (*to Simon, over the rain*) I'll get the other bike.

Dorcas runs off
SIMON   (*shouting back*) Fine.

Abigail gathers up as many things as she can and flees to the car. Brenda runs out with the kite and personal bits. Melvyn brings a rug and more items. On her way out, assisted by Len, Rita falls over. Simon bounds to help and assists Len with Rita to the car. Dorcas returns pushing the other bike. She is now very wet. She starts to push it towards the road. Before she can move very far, the drenched rat-like figure of Stafford slithers out to confront her

DORCAS (*shouting at him, above the elements*) Please, Stafford, get
out of my way.
STAFFORD (*shouting back*) I love you, Dorc.

They stand. An impasse

> *Simon returns, head down, blinded by rain. He gathers up the other
> bicycle. Only as he straightens does he see Dorcas and Stafford. Even
> in the rain, he manages to stiffen with fury*

DORCAS Stafford, please for the last time, get out of my way.
STAFFORD You can't leave me. I love you. I need you.
DORCAS Stafford.
SIMON Get out of her way.
STAFFORD You can't leave me.

*Impulsively, Stafford lies down on the ground in the path of her machine,
face down, prostrate. Dorcas looks at this pathetic sight. Then at the
wet figure of Simon, shaking his head rather contemptuously at this
craven behaviour. Dorcas decides whether or not to wheel her bicycle over
Stafford in order to reach Simon*

> *When Dorcas has gone one way or the other, with one man or the
> other, Abigail returns very wet to check that everything has been gath-
> ered up. She is stimulated by the prospect of a wet bicycle ride or
> resigned to dragging the prostrate Stafford to a more sheltered spot*

The Lights fade

*Should Dorcas have chosen to run over Stafford and go to Simon, Act
II Scene 1 Dorcas is now played. If, however, Dorcas opts to remain
with Stafford, Act II Scene 1 Abigail is played instead*

Act Two

Scene 1 Abigail

The same. Early September. Saturday, early evening, at about 7.30 p.m. A warm, pleasant evening at nearly sunset

Len enters from the road. He has the air of a man surveying the land. He looks about him, worried. He whistles, obviously to a dog. No response. He climbs the bank, whistling again

LEN   Trixie! Come on, Trixie girl. (*No response. After a swift glance around him, in a high unnatural falsetto*) Trix-Trix-Trix-Trix-Trix . . .

Melvyn and Brenda enter from the road. He carries a newly made home-built glider. Len stops calling abruptly

MELVYN   Good evening, Uncle Len.

LEN   What are you doing here?

MELVYN   Lost Trixie, have you?

LEN   Yes. She'll have smelt rabbit. Rabbit scent. Probably.

Melvyn whistles

No, she'll be away. She never lets the scent go. Never.

MELVYN   Right.

LEN   What have you got there, then? An aeroplane?

MELVYN   Supposed to be.

LEN   I see. (*He looks at it without favour*)

BRENDA   (*softly*) We made it.

LEN   (*sharply*) What's that?

BRENDA   I said, we made it.

LEN   Uh-huh. How did you get here?

MELVYN   On the bus.

LEN   I see. Well, I'll give you a tip. Just a friendly tip from me. If I were you, I wouldn't hang around here after dark on a Saturday night. All right?

90

MELVYN   Why not?

LEN   Because. That's why. Take her home and watch the football, that's my advice.

MELVYN   (*with a suspicion of sarcasm*) All right if we fly this, is it?

LEN   Suit yourself, it's a free country. You're free to do as you please. Don't behave in any manner so as to cause annoyance or inconvenience to other people, don't cause any undue or wanton damage to property and if that thing is on a control line – (*he nods at the plane*) – don't fly it above two hundred feet, or you'll have the Air Ministry to answer to.

Len laughs at this as it amuses him. Melvyn and Brenda just stare

   (*Getting more aggressive*) Have you got nothing better to do than that?

MELVYN   How do you mean?

LEN   I thought you'd have been sitting at home, racking your brains as to what went wrong.

MELVYN   What with?

LEN   With your exams, boy. All these medical exams your father spent money on for you to take. What happened?

MELVYN   I failed them.

LEN   Yes. You made a right Mafeking of it, didn't you? Broken your father's heart.

MELVYN   Dad doesn't care.

LEN   How do you know?

MELVYN   He said so. I went in to tell him. He said, how did the exams turn out, Mel? And I said, I failed, I'm afraid. And he said, oh well, fair enough. Better luck next time. And I said, I'm not taking them next time. And he said, oh well, fair enough then.

LEN   (*digesting this*) Yes, well he's a . . . He's not been himself. He was a fine doctor. Very little he couldn't put right when he set his mind to it. Rita's knee got the better of him, though.

MELVYN   Yep. See you, then.

91

Melvyn and Brenda go up the slope

LEN (*beckoning Melvyn back*) Here.

MELVYN (*coming to him*) Yes?

LEN Try and cheer her up a bit, will you?

MELVYN Why?

LEN Because she's like a mourner peeling onions, that's why. What's the matter with her?

MELVYN (*moving off*) She's all right.

Melvyn joins Brenda at the top of the slope. They disappear

LEN (*calling after them*) Remember what I said? Not too late. (*He consults his watch. Then, resuming his search, whistling*) Trix-Trix-Trix-Trix-Trix.

Patrick enters from the road

PATRICK (*surprised to see Len*) Oh. Good evening, Len.

LEN Ah, good evening.

PATRICK Very mild.

LEN Yes. Yes.

PATRICK Have you lost the dog?

LEN No, no. She'll be after rabbit. It's rabbit she'll have scented.

PATRICK Ah.

LEN Once she gets the scent.

PATRICK Yes.

LEN Taking a stroll, are you?

PATRICK In a way. In a way. Well. A stroll in the car, if you follow me.

LEN Ah.

PATRICK I find walking on the whole upsets me, you know.

LEN Oh yes.

PATRICK I mean, taken in any large quantities that is. Anything over, say, a hundred consecutive paces plays absolute havoc with my nervous system.

LEN Oh yes.

PATRICK Ever since my firm moved to a larger building it's posed endless problems for me.

LEN Uh-huh. Uh-huh.

PATRICK My secretary has to carry me everywhere.

LEN (*gravely*) Yes. Yes. (*Realizing the joke*) Ah. Ha-ha. Yes. Yes. Yes.

A pause

Yes.

PATRICK Actually I was looking for my wife. Have you seen her at all?

LEN Abi? Abigail? No, no. Gone missing, has she?

PATRICK In a way. She was on her bike, you see, wobbling along some B road. I was following in the car a few yards behind her. Then all of a sudden, she's gone. Pedalled off like mad down a footpath. Turned left and vanished. No hand signal, nothing.

LEN Dear, dear, dear.

PATRICK So.

LEN You were unable to follow?

PATRICK I was in the Merc, not a tractor.

LEN Yes, yes, quite. Pardon my asking, why were you following her in the first place?

PATRICK Well, I think it's a good thing for a husband and wife to get out together in the evening sometimes.

LEN What, her on a bicycle and you in the car?

PATRICK Well, each to his own.

LEN It sounds very peculiar to me.

PATRICK I had the sunshine roof open, for heaven's sake. We weren't being that unfriendly. I kept shouting encouragement to her. You know, 'keep going'. Rather like a rowing coach on a river bank.

LEN (*giving all this up*) Ah.

PATRICK Anyway, I daresay she'll turn up.

LEN Got lights front and rear, has she? On her bike?

PATRICK Oh yes, rather.

93

LEN   She'll be all right, then.

PATRICK   Are you on a walk or . . .?

LEN   Not really.

PATRICK   Oh. Business, eh?

LEN   Yes. Yes.

PATRICK   Oh. Well, enough said. I'm not interrupting a full-scale police manhunt, am I? You're not on the point of swooping, are you?

LEN   Beg your pardon?

PATRICK   Is there at present a police operation in progress which I as a member of the general public am hindering?

LEN   No.

PATRICK   Good.

LEN   The facts are, we are keeping just a little bit of a vigil, that's all.

PATRICK   I see.

LEN   There have been incidents on this common. Vandalism. Youths have been seen. Unnatural practices have been reported.

PATRICK   Unnatural practices?

LEN   Eye-witness reports.

PATRICK   But who is it who's been practising? Youths?

LEN   I wish I could say it was merely youths. If my suspicions are correct, it goes a lot higher than that.

PATRICK   Really?

LEN   That's a personal theory, you understand?

PATRICK   Good heavens. When you say higher, how high do you mean?

LEN   You name it. The sky's the limit, isn't it?

PATRICK   I mean – what? – Town Hall level, for example? That high?

LEN   (reacting sharply) What have you been hearing?

PATRICK   Nothing.

LEN   You can keep that under your hat to start with.

PATRICK   What?

LEN   You'll know exactly who I'm talking about, then.

PATRICK Who?

LEN I think you know. You'll know. We all know.

PATRICK But what sort of things are being practised?

LEN Well. Let's just say that the Vicar is also concerned. *Slightly humorous*

PATRICK You mean, he's involved?

LEN No, no, he's concerned. He's worried. (*Confidentially*) You've heard of a coven, I take it?

PATRICK A coven? You mean, witches, all that?

LEN That's what I think we're on to.

PATRICK Good gracious.

LEN Nude dancing and dead poultry, all that sort of palaver. Sacrifices, you know.

PATRICK And you're hoping to catch them at it, are you?

LEN Saturday night. A popular time, we reckon. Tomorrow is Sunday, you see.

PATRICK Well yes, they'd need a lie-in after all that, wouldn't they? Is this a big operation you're mounting then?

LEN Well, it was originally so intended as such but there have been administrative problems. A shortage of men. I sent a request to Slough requesting further assistance but they finally came through with a 'no'. Their idea of concrete evidence and mine obviously differs.

PATRICK Oh dear.

LEN It's the big dance as well tonight, you see. Divisional Police Dance.

PATRICK Oh, is it? Aren't you and Rita going?

LEN It wouldn't be lot of fun with her knee, would it? No.

PATRICK How is she?

LEN Middling to fair, middling to fair. (*Not wishing to dwell on this topic*) Anyway, so the operation is now down to what you might call, jokingly, a token force.

PATRICK How many's that?

LEN Me, a constable and the dog.

PATRICK Ah.

LEN Mind you, having said that, as the Army always has it, you can sometimes achieve more with a fistful of specially

95

handpicked men than you can with a whole regiment of recruits.

PATRICK   That sounds logical.

LEN   So.

PATRICK   All the same, between you, him and the police dog, you're going to have your work cut out, aren't you?

LEN   No, it's not a police dog. It's my dog. It's little Trix. She'll scent anyone long before we do. She's got a good nose on her. Could save us a lot of leg work. Excuse me. (*He whistles*)

PATRICK   She must be still chewing rabbits.

LEN   Yes. (*Calling normally*) Trixie. (*In a high voice*) Trix-Trix-Trix-Trix-Trix.

Patrick looks at him, startled

I have to do that. She's getting on, you see, and her hearing's going just a little. In the lower registers, that is. It's the deep voices she can't hear, you see. Men's voices, particularly. I mean, she'll always go running to Rita but if I talk to her normally, she won't hear me at all. (*Calling falsetto again*) Trix-Trix-Trix-Trix-Trix. She'll have heard that, you see.

PATRICK   She's not coming though.

LEN   No, well she'll make her own way. She's getting on. Still a good guard dog. She hears an intruder, she barks the house down.

PATRICK   Providing they're women, eh?

LEN   (*mildly amused*) Yes, yes. Well . . .

PATRICK   Yes, I think my wife's gone after a rabbit, too. Good luck.

LEN   Thank you – ah . . .

Murphy enters. He is a well-built young man in an anorak and heavy-duty trousers tucked into boots. He carries a loudhailer. He looks ready for combat.

LEN   There you are, Murphy, good lad. (*Seeing the loudhailer and taking it from him*) Ah, thank you for bringing that. This is Police Constable Murphy. This is Mr Smythe.

PATRICK How do you do?

Murphy nods

LEN You may have heard of this young man by reputation.

PATRICK Oh yes?

LEN He's made quite a name for himself in recent times. As a runner. He was the outright winner of the Pendon Cross-country last year. And next week-end he's going to win it again, aren't you? And break the record if I have anything to do with it.

PATRICK Jolly good.

LEN That's what I mean by handpicked, you see. There's nothing on two legs will escape this lad. He moves across this sort of terrain like a bloody whippet. (*To Murphy*) All right lad, lead on. We've got work to do. (*Quietly, to Patrick*) He's thick enough to start a timber yard but he moves like the clappers.

Murphy goes up the hill and off

PATRICK I think I'll take advantage of police protection and just scan the horizon with you. In case there's a lone female cyclist.

Patrick and Len moves up the hill

LEN (*calling*) Trix-Trix-Trix-Trix-Trix. I think she's run home, you know. I wouldn't be surprised. She's done it before. Oh well, she'll keep Rita company anyway. She's only sitting there at home with her leg up.

Melvyn and Brenda enter, meeting Patrick and Len: they are carrying the plane

Did it fly, then?

MELVYN (*examining the plane*) No, it's broken.

LEN Hah.

PATRICK   Good evening.
MELVYN   (*faintly surprised*) Oh. Hallo.

Patrick and Len go over the hill after Murphy

Brenda and Melvyn come down into the meadow

BRENDA   Are you sure it's broken?
MELVYN   Yes, it's a strut. Look, there.
BRENDA   Oh yes.

They examine the plane closely. We see them alone together for the first time: a glimpse of a very private relationship

MELVYN   You see, if I reinforce it here that should strengthen
           it.
BRENDA   Won't that upset the balance on the nose?
MELVYN   It shouldn't do. It's slightly tail-heavy anyway, I
           think.
BRENDA   If we modified the nose section slightly by adding
           another piece across here . . . Do you remember the other
           one we tried? That needed the same for some reason . . .
MELVYN   (*nodding slowly, considering*) Yep – yep – yep. Could
           do.
BRENDA   (*staring at the aerodynamic problem*) Yes . . .
MELVYN   Back to the drawing board . . .
BRENDA   Yes.

Abigail arrives from across country, pushing her bike

ABIGAIL   (*seeing them*) Oh . . .
MELVYN   (*offhand*) Hallo.
ABIGAIL   What are you doing here?
MELVYN   Mending this . . .
ABIGAIL   It's past your bedtime.
MELVYN   (*looking up to consider her*) What are you doing?
ABIGAIL   Having a bicycle ride, aren't I? Obviously.
MELVYN   Funny place to ride it.
ABIGAIL   (*irritably*) I've stopped now, for heaven's sake,
           haven't I? I've got off it.

MELVYN   So you have.

ABIGAIL   I thought you'd be at home looking through the Situations Vacant. Not flying – aeroplanes. I mean, really, Mel. I mean, honestly. What are you playing at?

Melvyn keeps his head down examining the plane

Mel?

BRENDA   (*softly*) Don't keep on at him.

ABIGAIL   What?

BRENDA   I said, don't keep on at him.

ABIGAIL   (*coolly*) I'm having a conversation with Mel on a family matter. I'm sorry. I don't think it has anything to do with you.

BRENDA   Oh yes, it has.

ABIGAIL   (*startled*) What?

MELVYN   (*quietly, not wanting trouble*) Bren . . .

BRENDA   Anything to do with Mel is to do with me.

ABIGAIL   I don't know how you work that out. All that's happened to Mel since you met him is he's stopped his studies completely and has just thrown away an extremely promising career. Reverting now, as far as I can see, to second childhood, playing with toys all day . . . Frankly, and I'll be absolutely blunt with you, I think your influence on Mel has been disastrous and the sooner he sees the back of you the better.

BRENDA   (*evenly*) I see.

ABIGAIL   Sorry, but it's best said, isn't it? (*Slight pause*) Well, at least we know where we stand. That's one thing.

MELVYN   (*who has not looked up from his plane*) I think it's this extra strut we put in that's doing it, you know . . .

ABIGAIL   (*more muted*) I'm sorry, it's just he's – our brother and we're fond of him and we want the best for him. I suppose. I'm his sister, I'm concerned, that's all. All right, I can see I'm making no impression at all on either of you. I'll say no more. I promise. Forget I spoke . . .

99

BRENDA   I see. I don't think it would be a very good idea for me to leave Mel now.

ABIGAIL   I can't see why not.

BRENDA   (*deliberately*) Well, with the baby coming . . .

A pause. Melvyn looks to see how Abigail has taken this. He then resumes inspection of the plane. There is the suspicion of a suppressed laugh from him

ABIGAIL   (*aghast*) Oh my God. You're not . . .? Mel? She's not . . .? Oh dear God. Oh no. Oh, this is . . . Oh heavens! Oh, for the love of . . . Well, I don't know what to say. I am absolutely speechless. I am sorry but for once I am absolutely lost for words. I just do not know what to say. What do you want me to say? I mean, I'm sorry I just cannot find the words. For the first time in my life I have to admit it, I am completely and utterly speechless. (*A pause*) What made you do it, Mel? What made you both do it?

MELVYN   Well, it's the result of a rather complicated chain of partly muscular, partly chemical changes that occur in the human body, particularly in the . . .

ABIGAIL   You know what I'm talking about. There's no need for it these days. You're both old enough to know that surely?

BRENDA   We wanted a baby.

ABIGAIL   Wanted one?

BRENDA   Yes.

ABIGAIL   But he hasn't got a job.

BRENDA   Then he'll have more time with the baby, won't he?

ABIGAIL   Oh, dear God.

MELVYN   It's all right, Abi, don't fret. We've got things lined up.

ABIGAIL   What doing? Flying toy aeroplanes?

MELVYN   That's a nice idea . . .

Patrick appears on the top of the hill

PATRICK   Well . . .

ABIGAIL Oh no.

PATRICK I wondered where you were.

ABIGAIL (*to Melvyn*) Why didn't you tell me he was here?

MELVYN I thought you knew he was here.

PATRICK (*indicating the bicycle*) I see you've dismounted your old grey mare.

ABIGAIL Only temporarily.

PATRICK What's she doing there? Turned her out to pasture, have you?

Abigail laughs tinnily. A pause. Patrick looks at Melvyn and Brenda

How are you two getting home?

MELVYN Bus.

PATRICK Want a lift in a minute?

MELVYN Oh, yes. Ta.

PATRICK (*tossing Melvyn his car keys*) Here, hop in then.

MELVYN (*taking the hint*) Oh, yes, right . . .

PATRICK Only please – Mel – do not tinker with my electric aerial, windows, sunroof, cigar lighter, air conditioning or interior lights.

MELVYN Can we play the cassette?

PATRICK Yes, all right.

MELVYN Have you still only got Mozart?

PATRICK Yes.

MELVYN Why don't you get something decent?

PATRICK Because Mozart is decent. He's the only music there is.

MELVYN (*shaking his head sorrowfully*) Oh dear, oh dear.

Melvyn and Brenda go off with the aeroplane to the car

PATRICK Now then . . .

ABIGAIL (*sharply*) Leave me alone. Please. (*She starts to pick up the bike*)

PATRICK You off again?

ABIGAIL Oh, go away, Patrick.

101

Patrick sighs, suddenly tired. He walks a little bit away from her

PATRICK (*at length*) It's getting awfully difficult this, Abi. It really is. I mean, I'm doing my best, honestly . . .

ABIGAIL What does that mean?

PATRICK I'm trying to understand. You've plunged into this thing with Simon. I mean, you're not exactly being discreet about it, are you? It won't be long before everyone knows and quite frankly, it's all making me look a bit of an idiot. I don't mind that. I really don't. As long as I know. But I would like to know. Is this simply a summer frolic or the big new love of your life?

ABIGAIL I'm – I've – I've had a bit to drink, actually.

PATRICK Ah, I see.

ABIGAIL Not a lot. I stopped at the pub. On my own. I was on my own.

PATRICK All right. Well. How long is this going on? How long do you plan to continue pedalling drunkenly round the countryside on a bicycle with a decidedly flat rear tyre?

ABIGAIL Is it? Oh – I don't know. I do not know. I love him. I love him awfully. He's everything you're not. He opens doors for you. And he shoves you into chairs and things.

PATRICK Oh, I see. Well . . .

ABIGAIL I mean, it's probably only because he didn't go to a smart public school like you did. And he's got lovely – well, he's got lovely manners in bed, too. If you want to know.

PATRICK In bed?

ABIGAIL Yes. He's – considerate . . .

PATRICK Shares the hot water bottle, that sort of thing, does he?

ABIGAIL (*supremely irritated*) Oh, Patrick, go away. Please. Just go away. Now. Please.

PATRICK I can't leave you sitting here, rolling drunk in the middle of a field.

ABIGAIL Please.

PATRICK   How are you going to get home?

ABIGAIL   I shall cycle.

PATRICK   Abi, you can't ride the damn thing properly when you're sober.

ABIGAIL   (*loudly*) Go away.

PATRICK   Are you meeting him?

ABIGAIL   What?

PATRICK   Lover boy. Is this a tryst?

ABIGAIL   Don't be silly.

PATRICK   I see. What are you planning to do? Meet up and pedal off together to a youth hostel? Better be careful which one you choose. Some of them don't like to see their young guests getting up to that sort of thing, you know. Or is it some small hotel you've discovered? That sounds more poss-ible, though I think you'll have trouble getting into the dining-room dressed like that. Unless you have an evening dress rolled up in your saddle bag. Is that it?

ABIGAIL   Piss off.

PATRICK   Oh, tremendous. Right, good night. If you do come home at dawn, as you have been known to, creep to bed quietly, will you? I have to be up early tomorrow. I want to oil the garage door.

ABIGAIL   Patrick . . .

PATRICK   Yes.

ABIGAIL   Don't be mean. Try and understand.

PATRICK   I am doing, I've already said that.

ABIGAIL   (*with difficulty*) You see . . . Oh, I don't know. It's all so muddled. I need all this. I need this adventure, this excitement. I couldn't simply go on running your little castle. It was getting so boring. I know, we had wonderful times, occasionally, but we always met the same people. And we'd started getting into the same routines. We watched this programme on Monday and we went to the pub on Saturday. I thought, God, I'll be old and I'll have done nothing. I'll be like all those other dreadful women with their shopping baskets on wheels having coffee in the back

of the delicatessen. And I'm worth more than that. A bloody
sight more than that.

PATRICK Dearest girl, if you'd wanted to be Amy Johnson,
you should have taken flying lessons. Now. You have your
affair and you ring me up when it's all over and I'll come
and pick you up.

ABIGAIL (*softly*) And if it doesn't finish?

PATRICK (*solemnly*) Then we'll have to – sort something else
out, won't we? O.K.? (*Rising suddenly*) My God, I'm being
absolutely marvellous about all this, you know. I am simply
beside myself with admiration for the way I'm behaving.

ABIGAIL Oh, Patrick, I am sorry. I'm an awful person.

PATRICK Yes, we knew that, don't worry. Go on, go to your
hotel. Gobble up your pre-heated dinner, charge straight up
to bed, you should get in a few hours' hard grind. Before
they knock you up by mistake at six a.m. with the man next
door's breakfast. Do you travel as Mr and Mrs or And
Friend?

ABIGAIL We don't do things like that. You're making it sound
very, very sordid and it isn't like that. There's nothing
underhand. I have been totally honest with you. You may
have behaved well but so have I. I've never lied to you.

PATRICK Only because you lie about as well as a ball-bearing
in a bunker.

ABIGAIL I have no idea what that means so I shall ignore it.
I can see what you're trying to do. Don't worry. I see
through you. You always were crafty. Like the way you
persuaded me to marry you in the first place.

PATRICK (*wearily*) What? What are you talking about now?

ABIGAIL And now you're being so deeply wonderful, aren't
you? You're making me sick. I wish to God you'd savage
me. At least I'd know where I was. There's so much forgive-
ness flying around, it's like being married to the Pope.

PATRICK Tell you what, I'll savage your bicycle, how's that?

ABIGAIL (*snarling*) You leave my bicycle alone. Go on, go
away. And for your information, there is more to Simon's

and my relationship than physical sex. We have things in common, things to talk about. He's witty, amusing, he's done things. He's seen things in Africa and places. God, he's exciting. Beside him, you're – you're like *coquilles St Jacques* and brown windsor soup.

PATRICK   Which of us is which?

ABIGAIL   (*savagely*) You are the soup, mate. You're sure as hell aren't the *coquille*. And we're not going to a hotel or a youth hostel tonight, so there.

PATRICK   You aren't?

ABIGAIL   Nope.

PATRICK   No?

ABIGAIL   No. We are not tonight, as it happens, actually going to bed together at all. In the true sense of the term.

PATRICK   (*intrigued*) Really?

ABIGAIL   Promise. So work that out. Good-bye.

PATRICK   You're going round to his place then?

ABIGAIL   What, with Brenda and his mother? Ha ha. You haven't met their mother.

PATRICK   (*baffled*) Well . . .

Melvyn returns from the car

MELVYN   How do you get those cassettes out of your tape machine when they've finished?

PATRICK   You press the button marked Eject.

MELVYN   Ah yes, but is there an override mechanism if that doesn't work?

PATRICK   Oh no.

MELVYN   It's all right. It's only Mozart. (*Humming a bit of K41*) . . . diddle-oo, diddle-oo diddle-oo-doo . . .

PATRICK   I'm coming, I'm coming.

MELVYN   O.K.

Melvyn goes back to the car

ABIGAIL   Good-bye, then.

PATRICK   Yes.

ABIGAIL   Well, go on. Or you'll miss something on television. Or down the pub. Old Stan in the snug will wonder what's happened to Mr Patrick. Usually buys me a pint, does Mr Pat, on a Saturday.

PATRICK   Oh, lay off, Abi, there's a love. It's not as dreary as all that, it really isn't.

ABIGAIL   Just seems it.

PATRICK   I don't think there's anything more we can usefully say, is there?

ABIGAIL   No.

PATRICK   I love you. Is that any good?

ABIGAIL   Not just at the moment, no.

PATRICK   Ah. (*He sits on the slope*)

Abigail remains in the middle of the meadow

ABIGAIL   Are you sitting there all night?

PATRICK   Maybe.

A silence: both in their thoughts. Then, a jingling sound is heard approaching. They both sit up and listen, trying to locate the source

Simon comes on from across country. He is laden. He carries a plastic water container, full. A small tent, a rucksack, jingling with cutlery, plates and supplies of food plus his overnight necessities. He also has a small gas camping fire, the sort that packs up with its own built-in saucepans, two rolled sleeping bags, a plastic washing bowl and a flashlamp, the type that has a red warning attachment

SIMON   Sorry, darling, the chain came off the bike and I had to . . . (*He sees Patrick*) Ah.

Patrick stares at him. Simon stands awkwardly laden

(*At length, to Patrick*) Hallo.

PATRICK   Hallo, there.

SIMON   I'm just – (*he searches his mind*) – I'm just – carrying a few things.

PATRICK   Yes, so I see.

SIMON   Bits and pieces, that's all . . .

PATRICK   Looks as if you're going camping. (*He laughs*)

SIMON   Yes. Doesn't it? (*He laughs very heartily*)

Abigail sits in the middle of them, getting hot and angry

PATRICK   Well, I'll be off.

SIMON   Oh, right. Must you? Yes, righto.

PATRICK   I think Abi's staying though.

SIMON   Oh, is she? Is she? Good. Splendid.

PATRICK   So you won't get lonely. Sorry I have to dash. Cheerio.

SIMON   Yes.

Distantly is heard the sound of Len's falsetto call

LEN   (*off, distant*) Trix-Trix-Trix-Trix-Trix.

SIMON   What on earth's that?

PATRICK   I don't know. Some woman calling her dog, wasn't it?

SIMON   Oh yes. Probably.

PATRICK   Good night to you.

SIMON   'Night.

Patrick goes

A silence until Patrick is well clear

Oh lord.

ABIGAIL   You didn't handle that very well, did you?

SIMON   Well, I could hardly . . .

ABIGAIL   Didn't you see the car?

SIMON   No, I came the other way. So I wouldn't be seen.

ABIGAIL   Well, you were.

SIMON   What are we going to do now?

ABIGAIL   It doesn't matter.

SIMON   But he's seen us.

ABIGAIL   So what, who cares?

SIMON   Well, surely he . . . I don't understand all this, I really don't. I mean, does he know?

107

ABIGAIL   Yes.

SIMON   Then he's behaving very peculiarly, isn't he?

ABIGAIL   He's a very peculiar man. That's why I'm with you, Simon.

SIMON   (*not altogether convinced*) Yes. O.K. Well. Gloss over that. As long as he doesn't want to sleep between us, I suppose, we'll have to accept the *status quo*. I'll stick your bike under the bush, shall I?

ABIGAIL   Thanks. (*Stopping him as he does so*) Oh, hang on. (*She opens the saddle bag and produces a bottle of red wine*) My contribution.

SIMON   Is that all you've brought?

ABIGAIL   Ah. (*Returning to the saddle bag*) Toothbrush. (*She produces it*)

SIMON   No night things?

ABIGAIL   Simon, I am not wearing night things. This whole evening's supposed to be natural and free.

SIMON   (*wheeling off her bike*) Yes, super. O.K. Won't be a tick.

Abigail, alone, examines the equipment he has brought dubiously

(*Off*) 'Way! Go 'way! Shoo, shoo.

Simon returns

ABIGAIL   What's going on?

SIMON   There was a repulsive fat old dog just about to pee over my bike.

ABIGAIL   Shoo it away.

SIMON   I did. It didn't appear to hear me. Anyway. Now . . . (*He looks about him*) Tent first, I think.

ABIGAIL   We don't need a tent, do we?

SIMON   You'll be glad of it at six o'clock in the morning when you wake up covered in dew.

ABIGAIL   Dew. Oh, that's wonderful. When did we last see dew?

SIMON   Don't know. It's not all that hot. (*He picks up the tent, packed very small*)

ABIGAIL   We can't sleep in that, it's minute.

SIMON   (*starting to unpack the tent*) Hang on. It does get somewhat bigger.

ABIGAIL   I want this to be a natural experience.

*During the following, Simon unpacks, lays out and finally erects the tent
at the foot of the slope. It is a small, modest affair just large enough
for two. It has the door at one end, facing away from the slope, and
a small ventilator window*

SIMON   It's a family heirloom, this is. Bren and I used to go
camping in it at the bottom of our garden. That was when
we were still young enough to be able to share tents
together. It's just big enough for two to sleep in. I mean,
you can get tents now, of course, with hot and cold in all
rooms, french windows and a musical cocktail cabinet but
that does seem to be losing the point, doesn't it, somewhat?

ABIGAIL   I'd get claustrophobia if I tried to sleep in this. I tell
you.

SIMON   Surely not. Weren't you in the Girl Guides, for
heaven's sake?

ABIGAIL   No, I was not. Dorcas was. But then Dorcas was in
everything that was going.

SIMON   Good for her.

ABIGAIL   My first memories of Dorcas are of a very small,
round girl dressed entirely in brown, eternally in search of
silver paper. (*Back to the tent*) We'll never get both of us to
fit into this.

SIMON   Hang on, hang on. You'll see. (*He struggles on with his
task*) It'll soon be dark, won't it?

ABIGAIL   (*ferreting about*) What's this thing?

SIMON   Oh that, that's a camping stove. Gas. Rather neat,
isn't it?

ABIGAIL   A gas stove?

SIMON   Yes.

ABIGAIL   Aren't we going to light a fire?

SIMON   Yes, if you like.

109

ABIGAIL We have to have a fire, a camp fire. It's not very romantic sitting round a gas stove, is it?

SIMON Probably not. But they're damned useful when it comes to brewing early-morning tea.

ABIGAIL Early-morning tea?

SIMON Yes.

ABIGAIL You're joking, surely?

SIMON What?

ABIGAIL You are, aren't you? You're joking.

SIMON How do you mean?

ABIGAIL Oh come on, Simon. This is an adventure. I mean, the next thing you'll have me doing the washing up.

SIMON (*laughing*) Well, I brought the bowl there, you see.

Abigail looks at him dangerously

No, that's mainly for washing. You've got no objections to us washing, have you? I mean, it's not too unnatural is it?

ABIGAIL No. As long as it's just for washing.

Simon continues to work on the tent

SIMON (*after a pause*) Abi.

ABIGAIL Mm?

SIMON Look – er – how many people is it that know? About us two, I mean.

ABIGAIL How do you mean?

SIMON Well, Patrick knows. And Dorcas knows. And Brenda and Mel know. Does your father know, for instance?

ABIGAIL He most certainly does not.

SIMON Oh good. And what about all these other people? Len and Rita, people like that?

ABIGAIL Not on your life. Of course not. What's wrong?

SIMON Well, I'm starting this teaching job in a week or two and I don't think this particular school would look too kindly on all this.

ABIGAIL Look, I'm not telling people. I don't know if you are.

If Uncle Len knew, it would be a disaster. And Pa would be very upset. He adores Patrick.

SIMON And there's no chance of any sudden whirlwind divorce, is there?

ABIGAIL No.

SIMON Just so long as I'm prepared.

ABIGAIL No. Patrick wouldn't do that. He'll do what I want. He always does in the end. Anyway. Poor old Pa. I'm afraid he's gone completely dotty now. He set fire to all his shoes the other day.

SIMON Ah. (*Standing back and presenting the tent*) There you are. What about that?

ABIGAIL (*looking at it without enthusiasm*) Well . . . You can sleep in it, I'm not.

SIMON (*easily*) We'll see. Fancy a cup of tea, then?

ABIGAIL No, I don't. God, you've suddenly got this obsession with cups of tea. I can't think of anything more boring. I mean, when you were out in the bush in Africa, you didn't all sit round drinking cups of tea, did you?

SIMON I never went out in the bush. I was thousands of miles away from any bush, actually. I never even saw a bush.

ABIGAIL Where did you live?

SIMON In a flat.

ABIGAIL How awfully dull.

SIMON It had a roof garden. That got pretty wild in the rainy season. That was about it. I did see a locust once. A dead one.

ABIGAIL Well, this is all one hell of an anti-climax, I don't mind saying.

The midges have arrived. They unconsciously swat at them as they speak

I thought we were going to rough it. I don't call this roughing it. Tents and continual cups of tea. We might as well be sitting on our carpet in the lounge.

SIMON (*getting needled*) Well, what do you want? For heaven's sake? There's no point in our being uncomfortable just for

111

the sheer hell of it, is there? I mean, even the chaps who go up Everest have been known to take the odd tent, you know. And I think some of them have actually been known to wear gloves. There's a distinct difference between roughing it and sheer suicidal lunacy.

ABIGAIL Yes, all right, all right.

SIMON Well, just don't keep on. I've done my best. I've been crawling about in the roof of our garage for most of the day, banging my head, trying to sort this lot out. I expected a bit of thanks.

ABIGAIL Now, don't start blaming me. You're the one who started all this hearty nonsense. You dragged me into it, not the other way round, may I remind you. You started all this bicycle riding. Don't start complaining if I want to do things properly.

SIMON I don't know what the hell you're on about, doing things properly.

ABIGAIL Well, look at it all.

SIMON All what? One tent with groundsheet. Two sleeping bags. One rucksack, containing two knives, two forks, two plates, two spoons, one teaspoon, one tin opener, two tin mugs, one packet of teabags –

ABIGAIL (*scornfully*) Teabags.

SIMON – half a pound of bacon, two eggs, salt, pepper, one small loaf, bit of butter, tin of milk, one tin beans, one bar milk chocolate –

ABIGAIL That'll do.

SIMON (*relentlessly*) – one plastic bowl for washing purposes only, one camping gas stove with pans attached, one towel, one torch and one spare battery and that's your lot. We're hardly equipped on a Himalayan scale, are we?

ABIGAIL (*pointing to the water container*) What's that then?

SIMON That's water. Fresh water.

ABIGAIL Well, that's unnecessary.

SIMON What do we do then? Sit round and wait for it to rain?

ABIGAIL   No. We could have got our water from the Trickle.

SIMON   From the what?

ABIGAIL   The little stream just down there. It's called the Pendon Trickle.

SIMON   Oh, is it? Well, have you looked in your Trickle lately? Because it's full of scrap iron. (*Indicating his water bottle*) Personally, I'm drinking from this. If you want to drink from the Trickle and risk swallowing bits of rusty refrigerator, you're welcome.

ABIGAIL   Well . . .

SIMON   I am now going to make up the sleeping bags in the tent and then, whether you like it or not, I'm going to get that stove going and have a nice cup of tea.

ABIGAIL   What about my fire?

SIMON   We'll see about your fire. It very much depends if you behave yourself from now on. (*He starts to move the sleeping bags towards the tent*)

ABIGAIL   You can leave my bag out here, please.

SIMON   Suit yourself. (*He crawls into the tent, taking one sleeping bag with him*)

ABIGAIL   (*moving her sleeping bag to another part of the field*) I'm putting mine here. Where I can see the stars, when they come out. (*She unrolls her sleeping bag and sits on it*) Oh, it's so peaceful here. Wonderful.

> 'So, we'll go no more a-roving
> So late into the night,
> Though the heart be still as loving,
> And the moon be still as bright.'

(*Trying to remember*) Who's that? Byron, is it? Or was it Shelley?

SIMON   (*from within the tent, with conviction*) Shelley.

ABIGAIL   Shelley, is it?

SIMON   Uh-huh.

ABIGAIL   No, it's not. It's Byron. It's Byron, not Shelley.

SIMON   Is it? I was never too hot on Byron.

Abigail sits. From within the tent, disturbing her peace, is the sound of a great deal of grunting and effortful sounds as Simon arranges his sleeping bag in the confined space

(*From within the tent*) Heeeup – hup . . . Hey – hup – ay.

ABIGAIL   What are you doing in there, for goodness sake?

SIMON   I'm trying to – hup – get this – round the tent – hup – post – that's it.

ABIGAIL   (*curiously, moving to the tent*) What's it like in there?

SIMON   Very cosy. Come in.

Abigail crawls cautiously half through the door

ABIGAIL   Oh yes . . .

SIMON   We can have a bit of fun in here.

ABIGAIL   It smells awful. It smells of old socks. You can't sleep in there. No-one could possibly sleep in there. (*She comes out into the fresh air*)

SIMON   I told you it's been in the garage for years. It'll air through.

ABIGAIL   It's quite off-putting. Ugh.

SIMON   It'll be O.K. Look, I'll open the window. (*He undoes the ventilator flap from the outside*) There you are. See?

ABIGAIL   Oh yes, that'll make a tremendous difference.

SIMON   (*still within the tent*) You'd better watch yourself or I'll come out there and get at you with a tent pole.

ABIGAIL   (*to herself*) Oh, lucky old me. (*Suddenly she giggles. Snatching up the stove, she runs up the slope with it. She throws it from her, presumably into the undergrowth. She returns, pleased with herself*)

SIMON   What are you doing out there?

ABIGAIL   Nothing.

SIMON   Right, that's settled. What next? (*He emerges from the tent, standing thoughtfully*) You know, just occurred to me. It's an odd time to think of it, I know, but in just a week today . . .

ABIGAIL   What?

SIMON   I'll be running the big race, won't I?

ABIGAIL   Oh, that.

SIMON   Yes. Straight through here. Pitting my skills against those of the redoubtable Constable Murphy.

ABIGAIL   Oh yes. Uncle Len's home-grown champion.

SIMON   I've seen him. He's quite good, you know. I think I can beat him providing I think out my ... (*Noticing the absence of the stove*) All right. What have you done with it?

ABIGAIL   Mmm?

SIMON   My gas stove. Where is it?

ABIGAIL   Now, you'll have to light a proper fire, won't you?

SIMON   What have you done with my stove?

Abigail points up the slope

Oh, my God. (*He snatches up the torch*) Where the hell is it? (*He climbs to the top of the slope*)

ABIGAIL   Somewhere in the bracken. You'll never find it in the dark.

SIMON   Oh, you ...

ABIGAIL   Find it in the morning.

SIMON   Oh, you stupid – prat.

Abigail laughs

You stupid – daft – half-witted – prat. Now we can't have any tea at all.

ABIGAIL   Light a fire.

SIMON   (*stamping down the slope*) No, really I'm bloody angry over that. I really am. (*He bangs down his lamp on the ground and stands undecided*) I mean, that's just a really prattish thing to do.

ABIGAIL   (*softening*) Simon, I'm sorry. Sorry. (*Cooing*) Won't you light me a fire, please?

SIMON   No.

ABIGAIL   Oh Simon, I'll boil you some tea if you make the fire. I promise.

SIMON   You can't boil me some tea.

ABIGAIL   Yes, I can.

SIMON No, you can't.

ABIGAIL Why not?

SIMON Because you threw our saucepans away with the stove.

ABIGAIL I did?

SIMON Yes.

ABIGAIL Well, can we still have a fire?

SIMON No, we can't, because that stove was self-lighting.

ABIGAIL And you didn't bring any matches?

SIMON Yes, I did bring some matches – but in order to keep them safe and dry, I packed them inside one of the saucepans which you may recall you threw away with the stove. So, that's that.

ABIGAIL Oh.

SIMON So. You wanted to rough it, now we're going to rough it. Unless you prefer to go home.

ABIGAIL Of course I don't. (*Penitent*) Oh, you're right. I am a prat. Whatever that is. (*She plays with the flashlamp*)

SIMON I better get the rest of this stuff inside the tent before you throw that away. (*He moves the rucksack inside the tent*)

The red section of the flashlamp begins to flash on and off

ABIGAIL Why does this thing flash on and off like this?

SIMON It's a distress signal.

ABIGAIL What for?

SIMON For people who've had their stoves unexpectedly chucked away. (*He disappears into the tent*)

Len's voice is heard again in the distance, calling his dog

LEN (*off, distant, falsetto*) Trix-Trix-Trix-Trix-Trix.

ABIGAIL (*switching off the lamp*) What is that noise? We heard it before.

SIMON (*sticking his head out of the tent to listen*) I don't know. It's a bit odd, isn't it?

LEN (*off, distant*) Trix-Trix-Trix-Trix-Trix.

SIMON (*bounding up the bank*) I'll have a look. (*He does so*)

ABIGAIL Anyone?

SIMON   No, it's too dark now.

ABIGAIL   Eerie. I'm glad you're here.

Simon comes down the bank

Perhaps it's part of these peculiar goings-on we keep hearing rumours about.

SIMON   What are those?

ABIGAIL   You know. One's always reading dark hints in the local rag. Strange goings-on on the Common.

SIMON   Oh yes, right. You mean, the witches and so on.

ABIGAIL   Yes. The funny Councillor What's'isname, he's something to do with it. Councillor Polegrave.

SIMON   Is he? Is he the one with the eyebrows?

ABIGAIL   Yes, he was nearly had up some years back but they hushed it up. He was seen one night chasing plump, white Town Hall typists in and out of the bushes in the Municipal Gardens.

SIMON   How do you know all these things, for heaven's sake?

ABIGAIL   Because I have coffee with Mrs Barnsley, the Chief Executive's wife every Thursday in the delicatessen. I hear all the scandal from her. She's wonderful, she knows everything.

SIMON   (*putting the washbowl in the tent*) You know, you're right. It is rather small in there. Well. What do we do now? Sit and look at each other?

ABIGAIL   That's no good. I can't even see you . . . (*Swatting*) Bloody midges – come over here.

SIMON   O.K. (*He sits by her on her sleeping bag*)

ABIGAIL   It's still being fun, isn't it?

SIMON   Um.

ABIGAIL   Go on. You've got to admit this is fun.

SIMON   (*catching midges vaguely*) Be a lot nicer with a cup of tea.

ABIGAIL   I bet you haven't even got a bottle opener, either.

SIMON   Oh yes, I have.

ABIGAIL   Well, then, we can have wine.

SIMON   Good idea. (*He produces a knife with many attachments and*

117

eventually finds a corkscrew) I think this will work. I've used it as a screwdriver, a bradawl, a miniature axe, a stone remover, a tin opener and a bottle opener, but I think I'm christening it as a corkscrew. (*Fetching the bottle*) Hey, this is very nice. Where did you get this?

ABIGAIL Oh, it's one of Patrick's.

SIMON It's a damned good claret. Does he mind?

ABIGAIL I didn't ask him, did I?

SIMON Crikey. Do you think we ought to?

ABIGAIL Go on.

SIMON But it's a sixty-two Latour.

Simon opens the bottle. Abigail sits watching him. She starts to hum to herself

(*Struggling with the bottle*) Ah-ha, that's significant.

ABIGAIL What is?

SIMON When you start doing that. Humming like that.

ABIGAIL Was I?

SIMON (*slyly*) Ah-ha. (*He opens the bottle*) There you go. Just a tick. (*He goes to the tent and returns with the mugs he has unpacked*) Here we are.

ABIGAIL Oh, surely we can . . .

SIMON No.

ABIGAIL What?

SIMON I'm not drinking a sixty-two Latour straight from the bottle. Sorry. There are limits.

ABIGAIL It's a good one, is it?

SIMON It should be. (*He pours*)

ABIGAIL Have you had it before?

SIMON No. I've dreamt about it sometimes. It's about thirty quid a bottle this stuff.

ABIGAIL Thirty quid!

SIMON At least.

ABIGAIL God, that bastard.

SIMON What?

ABIGAIL You know, he won't even let me stock up on ginger

118

ale. Thirty quid. That's immoral. You know, he puts the cheap bottles by the door. He thinks I can't be bothered to go right into that cellar. But I've got wise to that one.

SIMON Cheers, then.

ABIGAIL Cheers. (*She tastes it*) Mm. It's strong. Nice, isn't it?

SIMON Yes, it should have been left to breathe a little. Never mind. Good health.

ABIGAIL To us.

SIMON Yes.

They drink. A pause.

How's Dorcas these days?

ABIGAIL Dorcas? Oh, she's all right.

SIMON Still with her poet?

ABIGAIL Stafford? Yes. I can't imagine why. She claims she's slowly renovating him, but there's no outward signs of improvement as far as I can see.

SIMON Knowing her though, I think she'll probably achieve it. If she sets her heart on it. She's quite a determined character, isn't she?

ABIGAIL Yes, yes . . . Why are we talking about her?

SIMON Sorry.

ABIGAIL Talk about me, please, immediately.

SIMON O.K. Bit of a limited subject (*He laughs*)

ABIGAIL You'd be surprised. What did you mean just then?

SIMON When?

ABIGAIL About me singing. You said it meant something. Ah-ha, you said.

SIMON Ah well . . .

ABIGAIL What?

SIMON Well. It's just that you do sing.

ABIGAIL When do I sing?

SIMON When you're – when we're making love.

ABIGAIL Do I?

SIMON Didn't you know you were doing it?

ABIGAIL No.

SIMON   Oh yes.

ABIGAIL   What do I sing about?

SIMON   No, you don't have any words. You just make sort of musical noises.

ABIGAIL   (*amused and embarrassed*) Well. I never knew that. (*She thinks about it*) I don't.

SIMON   Yes, you do. You start off sort of – (*demonstrating*) – hmmm . . . hmmm – hmmm in the early stages as it were and then as things really get underway, it's sort of more – (*demonstrating again*) – la-la-la-la-la-la.

ABIGAIL   (*incredulously*) I don't.

SIMON   You do.

ABIGAIL   Patrick's never mentioned it.

SIMON   Perhaps he's tone deaf. (*He laughs*)

ABIGAIL   God, how awful. How awfully embarrassing.

SIMON   Oh, I don't know. It's rather nice really. Not so good in small hotel rooms . . .

ABIGAIL   So that's why you wanted to get me into a tent . . .

SIMON   Ah-ah. Now, now. You wanted the tent. I could see some of the advantages, of course . . .

ABIGAIL   (*laughing*) La-la-la-la-la-la.

SIMON   Yes, something like that. Only much louder.

They sit, drinking

ABIGAIL   Very dark now.

SIMON   Yes. Moon coming up though.

ABIGAIL   Yes. Oh, this is more like it.

SIMON   Good. (*He swats another midge*)

ABIGAIL   What are you thinking about?

SIMON   Oh, nothing that would interest you.

ABIGAIL   Everything about you interests me. Tell me.

SIMON   I was just thinking about the race next week.

ABIGAIL   Oh no, not the race again.

SIMON   I told you you wouldn't be interested.

ABIGAIL   You're with me in a field under the stars raring to go. And you're thinking about running races.

120

SIMON   Sorry.

Abigail kisses him. Simon goes to kiss her in return. Abigail lies back but is immediately in great discomfort

ABIGAIL   Ur . . .

SIMON   Mm?

ABIGAIL   Just a tick. I'm lying on something. A mallet. (*She moves it*)

SIMON   (*thinking again*) You see, the point about this chap Murphy . . .

ABIGAIL   Who?

SIMON   Murphy. This fellow I'm running against. His strength's in his start. He's got a damn good start. His finish, however, is suspect.

ABIGAIL   Well, we won't ask him to tea, will we?

SIMON   But I'm going to have to plan my strategy well in advance.

ABIGAIL   (*dreamily*) I dearly want to remember tonight. I want to make it something memorable. Oh Simon, let's go mad. Tell you what, you think of something to do and then I'll think of something to do and then we'll both think of something to do.

SIMON   (*none too sure of this*) Yes, O.K.

ABIGAIL   What are you going to do first?

SIMON   Well, I'm going to zip the sleeping bags together for a kick-off.

ABIGAIL   Brilliant.

Simon moves her sleeping bag to the tent. Abigail watches him dreamily. She starts to hum gently, something she continues to do from hereon in

(*Watching him*) You're all man, Simon.

SIMON   I hope so, yes.

ABIGAIL   I'll tell you what I'm going to do now. For your delectation. I'm going to dance for you. I shall take off all my clothes and dance for you.

SIMON   Hang on. I'm not Councillor Polegrave, you know.

121

ABIGAIL   By the light of the fire.

SIMON   What fire?

ABIGAIL   (*shouting angrily*) Oh come on, Simon, use your imagination.

SIMON   (*still working on the sleeping bags*) Sorry, I'll get into it in a minute. (*He emerges from the tent*)

ABIGAIL   You're about as romantic as a piece of knotted string aren't you? (*She goes down to the torch*)

SIMON   Oh come on, Abi. We've been sitting out here getting bitten to death by midges. We could've been in the tent, behind the insect net, having the time of our lives.

Abigail switches on the torch so that it starts to flash red, and plonks it on the ground

ABIGAIL   There. That'll do for a fire. All right? (*She starts to hum again, accompanying herself rhythmically as she dances*) Bom – bom – der – bom. Watch closely.

SIMON   Yes, I will. I can't quite make you out. Can you get a bit closer to the lamp?

ABIGAIL   Bom – bom – der – bom.

Abigail unbuttons her shirt in the manner of a stripper: eventually tossing it to the ground. Simon, sipping his Latour, begins to enjoy this

More?

SIMON   Yes, please. More. Goes well with the Latour.

ABIGAIL   Your turn, then.

SIMON   Eh?

ABIGAIL   To remove something. Come on.

SIMON   Oh God, Abi.

ABIGAIL   Come on, get it off. (*She starts to unbutton his shirt*) Bom – bom – der – bom.

SIMON   God, we'll get eaten alive.

ABIGAIL   (*throwing Simon's shirt to the ground*) That's better. Here we go. My turn. (*She continues to dance, removing her jeans. This turns out to be a difficult operation to do gracefully*) Bom – bom – der – bom ... Oh bugger these things, they always get

. . . (*She sits on the ground and struggles*) Don't look. You're not to look at this bit. (*Removing her trousers finally*) Right, you can look again now. Bom – bom – der – bom. *Voilà*, feast your eyes. Right.

SIMON My turn again, is it?

ABIGAIL Yes, your turn.

SIMON Yes, I was afraid it was.

ABIGAIL Get 'em off.

SIMON (*reluctantly removing his trousers*) We're very near the main road here, you know, Abi.

ABIGAIL Bom – bom – der – dom.

Distantly a dog barks

SIMON What was that?

ABIGAIL What?

SIMON Sounded like a dog.

ABIGAIL Never mind the dog. My turn. Don't miss this whatever you do. Bom – bom – der – bom. (*She reaches to unfasten her bra*)

Simon, despite his unease, is distinctly fascinated. Suddenly, the proceedings are further lit by two powerful torches. One from the direction of the road and one held by a figure standing on top of the bank. The comparatively deafening sound of the loudhailer cuts through the proceedings. Len's voice is heard, greatly amplified and distorted

LEN (*through the loudhailer*) This is the police. We have reason to believe you are at present indulging in unnatural practices. You are advised to stay exactly where you are.

ABIGAIL Oh my God! (*She stands, horrified*)

LEN This is the police. We have you totally surrounded.

SIMON (*urgently*) Run for it. (*Feverishly he begins to gather up his discarded clothes*)

LEN Stop them! Stop them!

Abigail screams and starts a frenzied search for her own clothes unsuccessfully

123

Get him, Murphy, get him, lad.

SIMON Come on, run like hell.

Len appears by the entrance to the road. Murphy hurtles down the slope

Murphy's charge causes Abigail to squawk in alarm, abandon her search for clothes and plunge for refuge in the tent. Simon, who has now found his clothes, runs round the other side of the tent and up the bank avoiding Murphy, who grabs at him vainly

LEN Go get him, boy. Go get him.

Murphy launches like a bullet after Simon. Simon disappears over the hill with Murphy in pursuit

Len, eager not to miss the chase, runs up the hill after them

(*Through his loudhailer*) There is no point in trying to escape. I repeat, there is no point in trying to escape. The policeman now pursuing you is a championship runner . . . Go on, lad, go.

Abigail's head comes nervously out of the tent. Her clothes seem too far away for a safe dash

Unseen by Len, a figure comes hurtling on from the road doubled up. It is Patrick

ABIGAIL Aah!

PATRICK (*pushing her back into the tent*) Get in.

ABIGAIL Patrick, what are you . . .?

PATRICK Shut up and get in.

Patrick and Abigail disappear inside the tent

LEN (*during the above*) Come on, Murphy, you can do better than that. Run, lad. (*He comes down the slope*) He'll get him, he'll get him. (*To the tent*) All right, come out of there. Let's have you. Come on. Out you come.

Patrick emerges, furious

PATRICK What the hell is the meaning of this? My wife and I are – Ah. Hallo, Len.

LEN Ah.

PATRICK I'm sorry.

LEN What are you doing here?

PATRICK Well, believe it or not, we've been trying to get a peaceful night. Only we've been terrified by naked madmen dancing round the tent.

LEN Ah, you saw him, then?

PATRICK We did indeed.

LEN And her?

PATRICK Yes.

LEN We're giving chase. Did they do anything? You know, unnatural at all?

PATRICK No, fortunately you arrived in the nick of time.

LEN Well, he's taken his clothes. (*Picking up the remaining garments*) Unless these are . . .

PATRICKS No, no, those look like Abi's. She was – well, we were, you know . . . (*He winks*)

LEN (*understanding*) Yes, yes, well . . .

PATRICK (*offering to take the clothes*) May I?

LEN (*handing them over*) Of course.

PATRICK Thank you.

LEN (*shouting at the tent*) Evening, Abigail.

ABIGAIL (*sticking her head out*) Oh, good evening, Uncle Len.

LEN I must say, I didn't realize this was your sort of thing. Tenting . . .

PATRICK Well, it was a spur of the moment thing, you know. We were sitting at home and we suddenly both became aware that our lives were getting into a rut, you know, always watching the same programmes on Mondays, off to the pub every Saturday . . .

LEN I know, I know, I see that. Well, you had fair warning there might be trouble round here, didn't you?

PATRICK I'll listen next time, I promise you that.

125

LEN Anyway, we'll soon catch this little flasher. He won't bother you again.

PATRICK Much obliged.

LEN We won't be going home completely empty-handed.

Murphy appears at the top of the slope. He is utterly exhausted. He clasps his side and bends double with the effort

Ah, Murphy . . . Murphy? What's happened? Where is he?

Murphy shakes his head

You don't mean he got away?

Murphy nods

How the hell did he get away?

Murphy shakes his head

(*Stunned*) Well, I don't know. I don't know at all. Well, I'm pole-axed. That's the only word. Pole-axed.

PATRICK Anything we can do?

LEN No, no, no. It's a police matter. Take my advice. You keep your flap buttoned up for the rest of the night. And next time, try and pitch your tent a bit nearer civilization.

PATRICK We will.

LEN Goodnight to you.

PATRICK Goodnight.

ABIGAIL 'Night.

LEN (*to Murphy*) Come on, lad. Not my night really, is it? I've had my best runner beaten and lost my bloody dog. Not my night. (*Calling as he goes*) Trix-Trix-Trix-Trix-Trix.

Len and Murphy go out to the road

ABIGAIL And what do you think you're doing?

PATRICK Amongst other things, saving your reputation. And mine.

ABIGAIL You were watching us?

PATRICK Only the last bit. Very good. Can I offer you a limited engagement at our next office Christmas party . . . All right, come on.

ABIGAIL What?

PATRICK Let's get home, quickly. I've had far too much fresh air already.

ABIGAIL Did you know?

PATRICK What?

ABIGAIL That Uncle Len would be patrolling about out here?

PATRICK No idea. I was just passing. I saw the big drive-in strip-tease signs and I thought . . . (*He breaks off as he finds the bottle*) My God, this is my sixty-two. Did you take this? Did you take my sixty-two? (*He sniffs the bottle*) Beautiful. God, that's beautiful. How could you do this to my sixty-two?

ABIGAIL (*handing him a mug*) Here.

PATRICK (*shuddering*) Ugggh! You're a barbarous creature. If I had my way, this would be a capital offence. You should be flogged mercilessly with cold, wet lettuce.

Abigail is humming to herself again

Are you getting dressed.

ABIGAIL No.

PATRICK Are you going home like that?

ABIGAIL Come and see inside my tent first.

PATRICK No, thank you. Seen one tent, you've seen them all.

ABIGAIL This one's got a window, look.

PATRICK Oh good. Don't fall out of it, will you?

ABIGAIL (*cooing inside the tent*) Patrick. (*She hums*) Patrick. (*A bare arm comes out of the tent doorway seductively beckoning*)

PATRICK Abi, what the hell are you doing?

ABIGAIL (*singing her siren's song*) Patrick – Patrick . . . (*Her arm disappears into the tent*)

PATRICK (*reluctantly moving to the tent and putting his head through the doorway*) Abi, if you don't come out of there and come home this minute, I'm going to . . . yurck . . .

He is yanked suddenly and violently into the tent, headfirst. He vanishes

(*From within the tent*) Abi, come on now . . .

Abigail's song is heard

Abi. Abi – now, Abi . . .

ABIGAIL   (*laughing a very dirty laugh*) Patrick.

PATRICK   All right, all right. That's it. All right?

ABIGAIL   All right.

PATRICK   Sure?

ABIGAIL   Mmm (*In a second, her song gets louder*) La-la-la-la-la-la . .

As Abigail finishes her song on a high, clear, drawn-out note Patrick's voice is heard joining with hers

BLACKOUT

Act Two

Scene 1 Dorcas

The same. Early September. Saturday afternoon at 2.30 p.m. A coolish day

A series of marker flags, red and blue, have been driven into the ground at occasional intervals down the slope, across the meadow and presumably leading to the road

Len enters immediately. He has about him a great sense of self-important urgency. It seems there is a small crisis. He is dressed in cap, top coat and boots. Round his neck, a stopwatch and whistle. He carries a clipboard. Around his sleeve an armband with the words RACE OFFICIAL inscribed on it

LEN (*calling behind him*) Right, follow me. Follow me. Quickly now.

Dorcas, Melvyn and Brenda come on behind him, practically running to keep up. All are dressed in similar vein. Dorcas in a coat; Melvyn in a thick jersey and carrying binoculars in an old leather case; Brenda in a jacket. Melvyn carries a home-made model glider

Now then, this is Checkpoint number seven. It is the last one before the finish. We shall need a steward standing here. I'd like you to take this one over, Dorcas.

DORCAS O.K. What do I do? Just stand here.

LEN I'll explain to you in a minute if I may. Let me just show this lad his position. (*To Melvyn*) You follow me. I need someone at Checkpoint five. It's just up here. (*He starts up the bank and pauses to straighten a flag, forcing it further into the ground. As he does so*) It's a crying shame this, you know. I mean, normally I'd have had twenty-five volunteers from among the lads. Now half of them I discover have had their leave cancelled. Nobody bothers to tell me.

DORCAS Oh dear.

129

LEN   I mean, I'm grateful to you for stepping in, but it's a crying shame.

DORCAS   Yes, yes.

LEN   There's eight of these checkpoints, you know. Every one of them needs a steward.

DORCAS   Yes, yes.

LEN   And I need six men at the finish and I'm still three men short.

MELVYN   Why has the police leave been cancelled then?

LEN   It's this peaceful demonstration in Slough, isn't it?

DORCAS   You expecting trouble?

LEN   In our experience there's always trouble at peaceful demonstrations. Half the tearaways in the districts will be there. And that is not all. I've had a dozen runners withdraw too, you know.

DORCAS   All policemen?

LEN   Well, half of them. The other half are demonstrating.

DORCAS   You've still got your star runner, I take it?

LEN   Who? Constable Murphy. Oh, yes, he's still running. I worked him a sick note. No, don't worry about Murphy. That boy-friend of yours is not going to get a walk-over, you know.

Melvyn kisses Brenda

DORCAS   We'll see. Simon's trained very hard.

LEN   He'd need to. (*To Melvyn*) Right, come on, boy, stop all that monkeying.

Melvyn stops

Did you bring your Dad's binoculars like I asked you?

MELVYN   Yep.

LEN   Good. Because I'm wanting you to cover quite a big area. Now, straighten yourself up. What have you got there?

MELVYN   It's a glider, look . . .

LEN   You're going to have no time for gliding, lad. Where's your armband?

MELVYN My what?

LEN Your official armband. Your insignia. What have you done with it?

MELVYN It's in my pocket.

LEN Well, put it on your arm, son, put it on your arm. The Press are here today as well, you know. I want this to look good.

Len goes off over the bank. Melvyn pulls a face at the others and follows him

Dorcas and Brenda stand for a moment

DORCAS Well. The rain's held off.

BRENDA Yes.

DORCAS I do hope Simon does well. He's been training hard enough. I've hardly seen him these past few weeks. He's run miles every day. Apparently this Murphy man is awfully good. Do you know him at all?

BRENDA No.

DORCAS Ah. (*She moves about whistling a bit*) I don't quite know what one does when one's stewarding, do you? I hope it's not too complicated. (*Pause*) Listen, you and Mel . . .

BRENDA Yes?

DORCAS Do you mind if I ask you?

BRENDA What?

DORCAS Well, he's my brother – my younger brother, and I suppose we've always felt rather protective towards him. Perhaps over-protective sometimes. I don't know. The point is, now he's failed his exams and as far as I can make out, he refuses to take them again, this means obviously he's given up any idea of medicine as a career. Well, fair enough. Father's upset but . . . Anyway, the point is, we're both – Abigail and I – we're both very worried he's going to drift aimlessly about – perhaps do something stupid – like rushing into marriage even. I think you'll agree he's got to have time to think clearly about his future. Without being affected by too many emotional considerations. He shouldn't

131

land himself with responsibilities. Not until he's ready. Don't you agree?

Brenda stares at her expressionlessly

Of course you're perfectly entitled to say this is none of my business . . .

BRENDA Yes.

DORCAS What?

BRENDA Well, I think I am. Actually. Entitled to say that.

DORCAS I see.

BRENDA I mean, frankly, I don't want to be rude or anything but I don't think it has the remotest thing to do with you whatsoever.

DORCAS Oh. Really? Well – actually, I know just now I said it didn't but I think it does. Number one, he is my brother. Number two, I don't think you're being a good influence on him. And, secondly, as his sister I think I am fully entitled to say so.

BRENDA Well, come to that, I don't think you're being an awfully good influence on my brother either. But if he wants to make a fool of himself over you that's his problem.

DORCAS I think your brother is probably old enough to know what he's doing.

BRENDA So's Melvyn, don't worry.

DORCAS I'm afraid I can't agree.

BRENDA Too bad.

DORCAS (*angering*) Now, you listen to me, you . . .

BRENDA I know what you and your sister think of me. I'm not completely and utterly totally dim as it happens. I've heard what you say about me and I've seen your looks and it doesn't bother me and it doesn't bother Mel, because he says you're both totally neurotic and out of touch, anyway.

DORCAS I beg your pardon?

BRENDA And for your further information, we shall be getting married very shortly actually because I happen to be two months pregnant. So gneeer to you too.

DORCAS   (*shaken*) Oh no. (*Pause*) Oh God. Now what's going to happen?

BRENDA   We're going to have a baby, that's what's going to happen.

DORCAS   But he hasn't even got a job.

BRENDA   He'll get one, I expect.

DORCAS   I don't know what this'll do to Father.

BRENDA   I can tell you that. It'll make him very happy. He already knows. Mel told him.

DORCAS   When?

BRENDA   (*shrugging*) A week ago.

DORCAS   Neither of them said anything to me.

BRENDA   I think they wanted it to be a surprise.

DORCAS   What for?

BRENDA   The wedding.

DORCAS   I don't know what's going to happen to you both.

BRENDA   We don't want much really.

DORCAS   Just as well.

BRENDA   As long as we're both happy.

Len returns down the slope with Melvyn

LEN   All right, have you got all that?

MELVYN   (*repeating*) Round the flag, down the dip, up the slope, through the stream, round the other flag . . .

LEN   No, no. Down the dip, through the stream, up the slope then round the flag –

MELVYN   – round the flag.

LEN   Now, about the third time round, some of them are sure to try it on so keep your eyes on them.

Melvyn kisses Brenda

DORCAS   I thought runners were all sportsmen and totally honest.

LEN   Not this lot. They're all as bent as hell. (*Seeing Melvyn kissing Brenda*) Blimey O'Reilly, you'd think he'd been away for a week.

133

MELVYN   We're going to get a cup of tea.

LEN   Well, the tea van's there. But two-fifty at your positions, please.

MELVYN   Yep.

DORCAS   Mel, I'd like a word sometime, please.

MELVYN   Yep. Sure.

Brenda and Melvyn go off towards the road

LEN   He's a dozy little punnet, isn't he?

DORCAS   (*shrugging*) Well.

LEN   And she's no better. Oh, she's all right to look at, but intellectually I don't reckon she can tell her fishcakes from her falsies quite honestly.

DORCAS   I'm sorry?

LEN   I beg your pardon.

DORCAS   In fact, I think she probably can. She's pregnant, did you know?

LEN   Yes, yes.

DORCAS   You did know?

LEN   Yes. Rita told me. I can hardly say I'm surprised. Right, now to get on. Checkpoint seven. (*Writing on his clipboard*) That's Dorcas. I'll mark that in. It's a crying shame all this, you know. I mean, it takes months to organize these things. I don't know if you appreciate that. I mean, as a start-off, you've got your officials, your catering, your first-aid, your toilet facilities. You've got the course to mark. A thousand things to think of, you know.

DORCAS   Yes, yes.

LEN   And now look at it. I mean, pardon me but it's a tragic fact that we're that undermanned that I've had to resort to five women.

DORCAS   (*stiffly*) Well, I expect we'll cope.

LEN   Oh, you'll cope. No disrespect, but some of these fellows are big rough lads, you know.

DORCAS   Well, I'm not going to have to fight them, am I?

LEN   No, no, no. Forget I spoke. Now listen – (*speaking as to*

a child) – I want you to stand just here. The start and finish
line is just through there by the road, you see. You see where
my finger's pointing? This will be the last checkpoint before
the finish. So it's an important one, right?

DORCAS Oh, dear.

LEN Now, don't panic. The runners start off by the road there
and they do half a mile of roadside running alongside the
B four-eight-one. Then before they get to the junction with
the main Reading road they branch off, cross the footbridge
that fords the Pendon Trickle, then they're cross country,
along Durkin's Ridge, through the spinney, down through
Hackett's Field, across the north-east corner of Grubb Farm
and then down towards us again – this time through the
Trickle, then up the other side of this slope here and then
they'll be in view and down this bank here. And this is
where you come in – down this bank. Watch this – (*he
demonstrates*) – around this flag here but it must be around
this way because it is a red flag and a runner always
goes to the left of a red flag and to the right of a blue
flag . . .

DORCAS Right of a blue flag.

LEN Have you got that then? He runs to the left of a red flag
and to the right of a blue flag –

DORCAS (*joining in with him*) – and to the right of a blue flag.
God.

LEN (*pleased at her confidence*) Now, you see what I mean. You
see what I mean. Now then, if you see anyone going to the
right of a red flag or the left of a blue flag, you will notify
me or an official umpire at the finishing tape and that
runner will automatically be disqualified. Just jot down his
number.

DORCAS It seems very drastic.

LEN A matter of feet can sometimes be critical. Even in a race
this length. (*Relaxing slightly*) Some of them, you know, they
play crafty. They muddy up their numbers to confuse the
stewards. If you see someone cheating and you can't read

his number, try and get a look at his face and we'll have an identity parade afterwards. (*He laughs*) Only joking, only joking.

DORCAS Ah!

LEN No, seriously, in actual fact, you should find it easier here. They'll be doing three laps, you see. Just a mile each lap, little under five miles in all. So by the time they reach you here, they're bound to have spread out, so the one thing you won't have is bunching trouble.

DORCAS Bunching . . .

LEN If it runs true to form, you'll probably get Murphy first, then a ten-minute gap, then your boy-friend – then another gap, then the rest of them. All right, any questions?

DORCAS Um. No. Left of red flag, right of blue flag.

LEN Correct. Got your notebook and pencil to record infringements?

DORCAS (*patting her handbag*) Yes, here.

LEN And your armband? Where's your armband?

DORCAS Oh. How stupid. I put it on my arm but then I put my coat on.

LEN Well, let's have it on view, my dear, let's have it on view. Otherwise you won't be accredited. You don't want that to happen, do you? (*Looking at his watch*) We've got a few minutes now but, please, I'd like you in position by two-fifty. All right?

DORCAS All right.

LEN We've got the loudspeaker van just along there by the start and finish so you'll be able to hear how the race is going if you're interested.

DORCAS Oh, good.

Simon comes jogging on in his tracksuit

LEN Ah-ha.

DORCAS Hooray! Hooray!

SIMON (*to Dorcas*) There you are. I wondered where you'd vanished to.

LEN She's now officially a steward of the course, so no collusion, please.

SIMON Ah, splendid. Just time for a bit of bribery then.

DORCAS Absolutely impossible.

SIMON (*testing her*) And which way round the flags do we go?

DORCAS Left of the red flag, right of the blue one.

SIMON Very good.

LEN All the runners arrived, have you heard?

SIMON Well, there's quite a good number jogging around over there.

LEN There should be twenty.

SIMON I say, who's that very old boy who seems to be competing?

LEN Ah, Major Lidgett has arrived, has he? I wondered if he'd make it.

SIMON Do you think he'll cope?

LEN Hah.

DORCAS Is Major Lidgett running this year again?

LEN No stopping him. Seventy-two years old, would you believe? He's been competing since it started forty-four years ago, only missing the war years.

SIMON Has he ever won?

LEN No, no. He's had a seventh, a twelfth and last year he was twenty-ninth in a field of thirty-four when he beat a man of twenty-three who was forty-eight years his junior. What is more, he has never failed to finish a race. Think what that means.

SIMON Incredible.

LEN Oh, he's got some running in him. He's got no speed now, not any more, but I'll promise you this he'll still be running when the rest of you are tucked up in bed, if need be.

SIMON Heavens.

LEN Having said that, I daresay you and Murphy'll lap him a couple of times. But he's a very popular competitor. He always gets a big hand from the crowd when he finishes.

DORCAS If anyone's still up, that is, eh? (*She laughs*)

LEN (*ignoring this cheap female joke*) Murphy's looking fit.

SIMON I don't think he'll last the course, will he?

LEN (*laughing*) Last the course. (*Feeling the turf*) The going's good, you know.

SIMON Seems firm.

LEN Could be records today, could be records.

SIMON I'll do my best for you.

Len laughs scornfully, then suddenly remembers

LEN Oh, by the way, a word of warning. The Press are about, so careful what you say.

DORCAS Why?

LEN Well, they'll be sniffing, you know. Sniffing for tittle-tattle. It's always best, we've found, to treat them with respect and kid gloves and tell them nothing except through official channels. So all interviews after the race handled officially through me, all right? We've had a bit of trouble in the past. Right, I must sort the rest out. Two-fifty.

DORCAS Yes, Uncle Len.

LEN (*to Simon*) Don't miss the start.

SIMON No chance.

Len goes off to the road

I've been thinking. The thing with Murphy is, from what I've heard, he always gets off at a cracking start but if he's got one weak point it's his finish. If I can hang on to him for the first couple of laps, I think I might nail him.

DORCAS Good.

SIMON Depends if I can stick with him.

DORCAS Look, I don't want to spoil your race but do you know what I've just heard?

SIMON What's that?

DORCAS Mel, my idiot brother, has succeeded in making your sister pregnant.

SIMON Yes, that's a bore, isn't it?

DORCAS Did you know?

SIMON Yes, she told me.

DORCAS Oh, God.

SIMON Actually they're taking it very calmly. I mean, in their position I think I'd . . .

DORCAS Everybody knew except me.

SIMON Oh, I shouldn't think so.

DORCAS It's a bit much. If Abi knows, I'll be furious. It means nobody trusts me.

SIMON (*kissing her*) Come on.

DORCAS (*irritable*) What?

SIMON Come on, kiss.

Dorcas kisses him very half-heartedly

Oh all right, forget it. (*He moves away*)

DORCAS Well. It's the first time I've seen you for days, isn't it?

SIMON Untrue. I'm the man who's sleeping with you, remember.

DORCAS That's not much good. You're asleep then.

SIMON Ah-ah-ah. Unfair.

DORCAS Yes, you are. You're clapped out with all this running all day.

SIMON And if you must work all hours of the night reading the traffic news.

DORCAS I shan't be doing that much longer. Not unless Father improves. He's going completely crackers, I think. He was sitting in the bathroom the other morning talking to his feet.

SIMON Oh lord. Anyway, you've always said if I may remind you that the reason you loved me in the first place was because I was – fit . . .

DORCAS One of the reasons.

SIMON That's what you said to me.

DORCAS One only of the reasons. I mean, I didn't fall in love with you just because you were fit. That's not a reason for

139

falling in love. I found it attractive, pleasing, yes. But I didn't fall in love with your calf muscles.

SIMON   Oh, disappointing. I thought you women went for that.

DORCAS   Hardly.

SIMON   What are all those he-man magazines doing then? I thought you all went out and bought them.

DORCAS   Those? They're not for women.

SIMON   Aren't they? Who then?

DORCAS   They're for men, aren't they?

SIMON   Men!

DORCAS   I've always assumed so. They don't interest me.

SIMON   (realizing) Really? Good lord. I never knew that. Good heavens. That's interesting.

DORCAS   Wow, you're all man. Simon. You really are.

SIMON   (not hearing this) Pardon?

DORCAS   Nothing.

SIMON   So I'm wasting my time with all this, am I?

DORCAS   How do you mean?

SIMON   Well, according to you all I can hope to do rushing about like this is excite the other runners.

DORCAS   Oh, really.

SIMON   I was only doing it for you.

DORCAS   Oh please, don't start that one.

SIMON   I was.

DORCAS   Oh, Simon, come on.

SIMON   Why else?

DORCAS   Well . . .

SIMON   Why else? Eh?

DORCAS   Because – well, because your vanity was challenged.

SIMON   Vanity? I haven't got any vanity.

DORCAS   You want to beat this man Murphy because Uncle Len says you can't.

SIMON   Don't you worry about that. I'll beat Murphy. I can beat Murphy hopping on one leg.

DORCAS   Well, that's why you're running. If you want to know. So don't blame it on me.

SIMON   I don't know what we're arguing about I'm sure.

DORCAS   We're not arguing. I'm telling you why you're running in this ridiculous race and why I'm spending my Saturday afternoon off standing in a field wearing an armband and watching flags.

Len's voice is heard off, testing the loudspeaker equipment

LEN   Testing one, two, three, four, testing . . . .

Dorcas looks at her watch

SIMON   I mean, if you'd rather I was like what's'isname . . . .

DORCAS   What's'isname?

SIMON   That little squirt you were with. What's his name?

DORCAS   Stafford.

SIMON   Yes. If you'd like me like him just say the word. Lying on the sofa smoking two hundred fags a day.

DORCAS   Who?

SIMON   Isn't that what you told me he did? Damn sight less effort, I can tell you.

DORCAS   I wonder what he's doing now.

SIMON   Setting fire to someone else's sofa, I should think. Who cares.

DORCAS   You know, the last time I saw him was here at that picnic.

SIMON   *(remembering him)* Hah.

DORCAS   I'm sorry, Simon, I can't help worrying about him now and then.

SIMON   Why bother?

DORCAS   Well, he was so – hopeless.

SIMON   Very good description. Hopeless.

DORCAS   *(dreamily smiling)* The only hope for someone like me with pigeon toes is that one day, I'll be carried off feet first in a flight of my own fancy.

SIMON   Eh?

DORCAS   Poem.

SIMON   Oh, Shelley or Shakespeare?

141

DORCAS Neither. It's something Staff wrote on my ceiling once. When I was feeling depressed.

SIMON I'm not surprised if he scrawled all over your ceiling. Not even a very good poet, was he? I mean, if you're going to do things like that, you've got to make sure you're Michelangelo first. Not some offensive little erk with pigeon toes.

DORCAS (*rallying*) Don't be so miserable.

SIMON Miserable?

DORCAS Well, you don't have to knock people all the time.

SIMON Eh?

DORCAS It's as if you're always trying to prove something.

SIMON What?

DORCAS Well . . .

SIMON What?

DORCAS Well, you're always belittling people. I think in the hope that it'll make you feel taller.

SIMON Is that another of his poems?

DORCAS No.

SIMON Well, it's rubbish anyway.

DORCAS I don't think it is.

SIMON It's an absolute load of sheep's droppings. I'm not worried about the little maggot.

DORCAS There you go again, belittling him.

SIMON (*getting quite angry*) I am not belittling him. He is already little. It is not possible to belittle anyone who is already as small as he is. It's like trying to insult a dwarf by calling him short. It can't be done. (*Realizing he is angry, and getting angrier*) Why are you doing this to me?

DORCAS What?

SIMON Annoying me like this.

DORCAS I'm sorry.

SIMON I have a race to run in a minute.

DORCAS I'm sorry.

SIMON Against a flat-footed police constable with an I.Q. of ten who's . . . (*Breaking off; furiously*) All right, all right, I'm doing it again, is that it?

DORCAS Yes.

SIMON (*shouting*) Good. I meant to.

DORCAS Sssh.

SIMON My God. You are one of the only two people I have ever known who could make me angry. Do you know that? The other was a salesman I worked with in Africa. I mean, you're not as bad as him but sometimes you run him pretty close, I can tell you.

DORCAS What did he say to you? To annoy you?

SIMON Who?

DORCAS This salesman in Africa.

SIMON I forget now. Nothing. I don't want to talk about it. He used to hide my briefcase. Things like that. Childish things. So-called jokes. You know.

DORCAS (*solemnly*) I see. No, that couldn't have been much fun.

SIMON It wasn't. That's one of the reasons I'm glad I came back.

DORCAS You don't really like jokes much anyway, do you?

SIMON I only like jokes if they're funny. Nothing abnormal in that, is there?

DORCAS No. That's awfully normal, Simon.

SIMON Oh good. I mean, just in case you wanted to get at me some more.

DORCAS I'm sorry. I just want everything to be perfect, I suppose. I think that's my trouble.

SIMON I thought that was Abi who always wanted that.

DORCAS No. Abi expects everything to be perfect. That's a bit different.

SIMON Sounds the same to me in the long run.

Under the following, Len's voice is heard over the loudspeaker system on the van, loud initially then fading down under

LEN Good afternoon, ladies and gentlemen, boys and girls. Welcome once again to the Pendon cross-country event. This afternoon will be the thirty-eighth time this race has been run and will contain a field of twenty runners. The

143

event as normal will be competed over three laps comprising a total distance of five miles three hundred and twenty-four yards, mostly over the rough and taxing terrain of Pendon Common. Among the competitors this afternoon, we have last year's winner Police Constable John Murphy, running in this his fourth consecutive year. John Murphy, number seventeen. Among the other contestants, we are pleased to welcome for the thirty-eighth time, Major George Lidgett: now, and I know he won't mind my saying this, seventy-two years of age and still running strong. Last year, Major Lidgett finished twenty-ninth in a field of thirty-four. So you can see there is still a lot of running left in him. He will be competing in the number twenty-three shirt. Finally, a newcomer who promises to provide a healthy challenge to the leaders, Simon Grimshaw, running in the number eight vest. Without further ado, I'm going to ask all the entrants to gather on the starting line now, please, ready for the start. Our official starter this afternoon, as usual, will be Group Captain R. W. Brodie and the finishing judges Messrs Bradley, Townsend, Cliff and Motherwell. Would the contestants please take their places for the start? Thank you.

As the above rumbles on interminably –

DORCAS   Is something happening?

SIMON   (*sulky*) Probably.

DORCAS   Well, hadn't you better be getting ready? I mean, I know you're confident but it might be as well to start with the rest of them.

SIMON   And I'll have less of that too, if you don't mind.

DORCAS   What?

SIMON   Sarcasm. I can't stand sarcasm.

DORCAS   Oh, go and run your race, for heaven's sake.

SIMON   I mean, maybe you're right. Maybe I am egocentric. I say, maybe. But if I am then I'm damn sure you are.

DORCAS   I didn't say you were egocentric.

SIMON   Building myself up at the expense of others . . .

DORCAS   That isn't necessarily . . .

SIMON Well, what else is it? Isn't that what you call egocentric?

DORCAS Not entirely

SIMON Just answer my question, please. Are you or are you not accusing me of being egocentric?

DORCAS You are not more egocentric than most people.

SIMON (*shouting at her*) I don't care about other people. I'm not interested in them. I am talking about me. Do you consider me egocentric?

DORCAS (*angry now, too*) Will you kindly not shout and scream at me.

SIMON If you don't behave yourself, I'll do a damn sight more than shout. I'll take this flag and tan your backside with it. So there.

DORCAS You do that and I'll put it back in the wrong place and disqualify you.

Simon steps back, momentarily baffled

Murphy enters, jogging. He is a powerfully built young man with the grim dedication of a serious runner. He wears running vest with the number 17 pinned back and front. He still wears his tracksuit bottoms

Simon and Dorcas draw apart from their near-violent encounter
(*Brightly*) Good afternoon.

Murphy nods but keeps his eyes gimlet-like on Simon, as if appraising a felon. There is a stare-out for a moment as Simon glares back and then Murphy jogs off again, having seen his opposition.

Murphy goes

Was that Murphy?

SIMON That's Murphy.

DORCAS Looks rather impressive, doesn't he?

SIMON He's all right. He looks better when he's got his walking stick. (*He begins to remove his tracksuit, moving towards the start*)

145

DORCAS Good luck.

SIMON (*smiling and winking at her, affectionately*) You need a bit of taking in hand, I can see that.

DORCAS (*wincing but managing to smile*) Good luck.

SIMON Yes.

Simon jogs out. As he goes, he passes Melvyn returning with Brenda in tow, still carrying the glider

MELVYN Good luck.

SIMON (*off*) Ta.

MELVYN (*to Dorcas*) Do you know what you're doing then?

DORCAS Yes, I think so.

MELVYN More than we do. We're just going to trip up Murphy as he comes past.

Melvyn and Brenda start up the slope

DORCAS Mel.

MELVYN Yep?

DORCAS Just a second, would you?

MELVYN What? (*He stops somewhat reluctantly*)

After a look between them, Brenda moves on

DORCAS Why didn't you tell me, Mel? About Brenda?

MELVYN Oh, that.

DORCAS Yes.

MELVYN Well . . .

DORCAS I mean, it's a bit hurtful, Mel.

MELVYN (*uneasily*) Yes, well – I thought you might have gone on a bit.

DORCAS I see.

MELVYN So. (*He looks at her, shrugs then runs up the slope*)

DORCAS Mel?

Melvyn turns

Did you tell Abi?

MELVYN No fear. She'd've gone on even more, wouldn't she?

DORCAS (*smiling*) Yes.

Melvyn and Brenda go out over the hill

The sound of the starter is heard off. Group Captain Brodie getting the race underway, finishing with the starter's pistol. Dorcas, alone, does her own start and runs round her flags

Hup, hup.

An almost unrecognizable Stafford enters. He wears an impressive sporting cap and a smart expensive coat

STAFFORD Hallo.

DORCAS (*caught in her running, but not recognizing him*) Oh, hallo. Sorry, I was just . . . My God. Stafford?

STAFFORD Yes.

DORCAS Staff, what are you . . .? Heavens. Staff, you look – you look so different.

STAFFORD Yes.

DORCAS How are you?

STAFFORD I'm – I'm doing fine.

DORCAS Why are you here? Didn't you go home to Leicester?

STAFFORD No – I – well – I did what you said once. You said, write to the Arts Council, for money, you know. For my writing. So I wrote to them. But they said no. So then I got this job, you see.

DORCAS What job?

STAFFORD With the *Gazette*.

DORCAS The *Pendon Gazette*?

STAFFORD Yeah.

DORCAS As a reporter?

STAFFORD Yeah.

DORCAS I didn't know . . .

STAFFORD Well, I wanted to get the job first and surprise you. You know.

DORCAS Well, Wow. You look very smart.

STAFFORD Well, I'm doing weddings and funerals, you see.

147

DORCAS   Why are you here?

STAFFORD   I'm writing about the race. I do Sports as well, sometimes. On Saturdays, I thought you might be here with . . .

DORCAS   Simon.

STAFFORD   Simon, yeah. I was actually looking for someone who might be able to help me with my report. Get some terms. Technical terms, you know.

DORCAS   What, about running?

STAFFORD   Yes.

DORCAS   Well, you could ask Uncle Len. Have you seen him yet?

STAFFORD   Yes.

DORCAS   What did he say when he saw you?

STAFFORD   I don't think he remembered me.

DORCAS   No.

STAFFORD   He kept calling me 'squire'. The berk. You don't happen to know any terms, do you?

DORCAS   Running terms? Er – well – flags.

STAFFORD   (nodding) Yes.

DORCAS   Runners. Er – start – finish . . .

STAFFORD   (consulting his notebook) Yes, I think I've got most of those down here.

DORCAS   Well, I'm a steward of the course.

STAFFORD   (nodding reporter- like) Uh-huh . . . (He writes painfully in his notebook)

DORCAS   And this is Checkpoint seven.

STAFFORD   Uh-huh, uh-huh.

DORCAS   What else? Oh yes. You go left round the red flags and right round the blue ones.

STAFFORD   Steward of the course, and checkpoint . . .?

DORCAS   Checkpoint seven. Seven.

STAFFORD   (closing his notebook, seemingly satisfied) Yes, I think I can build a story round that O.K.

DORCAS   (suspiciously) Stafford, are they printing the bits you write for them?

148

STAFFORD   Well, possibly.

DORCAS   What do you mean, possibly?

STAFFORD   I only started on Friday.

DORCAS   What Friday yesterday?

STAFFORD   Yes. I meant to start on Monday only I was in bed. (*Explaining*) Ill.

DORCAS   So this is your first job?

STAFFORD   Yes, first assignment.

DORCAS   (*very doubtfully*) I hope this works out for you, Stafford.

STAFFORD   Yes.

The loudspeaker is heard again, off

LEN   (*off, over the loudspeaker*) Just to keep you posted, ladies and gentlemen, boys and girls. The athletes should just about now be turning off the B four-eight-one and in another minute or so our spotters should be able to glimpse the front runners moving along Durkin's Ridge, preparatory to moving down into Hackett's Field. Thank you.

DORCAS   Shouldn't you be watching?

STAFFORD   No, no. I want to get the atmosphere first.

DORCAS   That's where the finish is, you see. They'll be coming down this hill soon. They have to do three laps, you see.

STAFFORD   (*not interested by this*) Ah.

DORCAS   How's the poetry? Have you been writing lately?

STAFFORD   No.

DORCAS   Have you been on the novel?

STAFFORD   No, no. I've stopped all that.

DORCAS   Stopped writing?

STAFFORD   Yes.

DORCAS   You can't.

STAFFORD   I have.

DORCAS   Stafford, that is criminal. You can't give up your writing. I absolutely forbid it. You have a great talent. A fine talent, so let's not hear any more of that nonsense. Do you hear me?

149

STAFFORD How are you?

DORCAS I'm fine. Do you hear me?

STAFFORD Yes. Anyway, so here I am.

DORCAS Yes.

STAFFORD Back again.

DORCAS Yes.

STAFFORD So. Hi.

DORCAS (*suspiciously*) What are you talking about?

STAFFORD You and me.

DORCAS I thought that's what you meant. I'm permanently with Simon now.

STAFFORD Ah yes, but that was before.

DORCAS Before what?

STAFFORD Before I got this job and a suit and money and everything. See? So now you have to say yes.

DORCAS Oh, don't be so totally daft.

STAFFORD O.K. What else do you want? Do you want me to run in this race, is that it? O.K. I'll run in this race. (*He starts to take his coat off*)

DORCAS Stafford!

STAFFORD Look, why else do you think I've sold out like this? I've only sold out for your sake.

DORCAS Why does everyone keep doing things for my sake?

STAFFORD What else do you want?

Melvyn appears on the ridge with his binoculars

MELVYN (*excitedly*) I can see the first two. It looks like Murphy with Simon close behind him.

DORCAS Oh. Good.

MELVYN They'll be here soon. Oh, hi there, Staff. Didn't recognize you.

STAFFORD Hi, Mel.

MELVYN Win the Pools?

STAFFORD No.

MELVYN Must get back.

Melvyn goes

DORCAS   (*suddenly amused*) Oh Staff, you really are ridiculous.

STAFFORD   Ha!

DORCAS   What are you doing working for the *Pendon Gazette*? I mean, honestly. And more important what made them take you on?

STAFFORD   I think I had good references.

DORCAS   Who from?

STAFFORD   Well, your father.

DORCAS   Pa wrote you a reference?

STAFFORD   Yes.

DORCAS   Well, he's mad anyway.

STAFFORD   Yes, he must be. He made out I was Lord North-cliffe. Then I told this assistant editor I'd had this very sporting youth, you see.

DORCAS   (*giggling*) What?

STAFFORD   I said I'd been given a trial for Manchester United, only I had to . . . (*He breaks off, laughing; a strange honking sound*)

DORCAS   Why are you laughing?

STAFFORD   (*still laughing*) I said I had to quit the game because of my pigeon toes.

DORCAS   (*helpless*) You didn't?

STAFFORD   And he believed me.

DORCAS   Oh, dear God.

MELVYN   (*off*) Hooray.

Dorcas and Stafford lie on the bank, laughing.

Murphy appears at the top of the slope, glistening, breathing heavily and working hard. He descends the slope with much silent panting and grunting

DORCAS   (*springing up*) Oh no. (*She runs to her post. As she does so*) Don't let Simon see you.

Stafford obligingly stands well clear of the runners, his cap pulled well down

(*Waving Murphy along*) To your left round the red flags, right round the blue flags. Thank you.

Murphy looks at her dangerously

Simon appears only a few yards behind at the top of the hill

(*Seeing him*) Oh, hooray, hooray.

Simon does not acknowledge this, looking grim and determined

(*Also getting business-like*) To your left round the red flags, right round the blue flags. Thank you.

Murphy goes off during the above. Simon now follows him

Did he see you?

STAFFORD   I don't think so.

DORCAS   Good, because I don't think he'd be too pleased at present.

STAFFORD   Yes. Anyway, then I told this editor . . .

DORCAS   Stafford, shouldn't you be writing any of this down? You know, Constable Murphy after one lap was being hotly pursued by Simon Grimshaw . . .

Stafford does not seem to think so

Melvyn appears at the top of the slope

MELVYN   Did you see that? Did you see that?

DORCAS   Mel, get back.

MELVYN   There's no-one coming yet, it's all right.

Melvyn goes.

The loudspeaker is heard off

LEN   (*off, on the loudspeaker*) The two runners coming through at the moment leading the field, perhaps predictably, Number seventeen, John Murphy, who has just registered an official first lap time of eight minutes thirty-four point four seconds which constitutes a new first lap record for this particular course. Close behind him in Number eight, Simon Grimshaw in a time of eight minutes forty-two point one seconds. So as you can see, there is very little in it at present. Thank you.

DORCAS Isn't that good? Sorry, you were saying?

STAFFORD Then I told this editor that I went from there into teaching, you see. P.E. and so on.

DORCAS Why P.E.?

STAFFORD It sounded good and then I got offered this job, you see, with this firm in Africa that sold machine tools.

DORCAS Stafford. Did you mention Simon's firm?

STAFFORD Yes. B.L.M. Ltd. I remembered it.

DORCAS But they might check.

STAFFORD That's all right. I gave them his name as well.

DORCAS Just a second. You've told the *Gazette* that your name is Simon Grimshaw?

STAFFORD Yes.

DORCAS For heaven's sake, Stafford, they're bound to find out you're not. What happens when they find out you're Stafford Wilkins?

STAFFORD That's all right, I told them that Simon Grimshaw was just my nom de plume.

DORCAS And they believed that?

STAFFORD Well, it sounded reasonable. Nobody in his sane mind would write under the name of Stafford Wilkins.

DORCAS All the same it's going to be very confusing when you report this race, isn't it? Simon Grimshaw reports on Simon Grimshaw.

STAFFORD That's O.K. I shan't mention him, don't worry.

Dorcas gives up

Len enters from the starting area, looking worried

LEN Excuse me . . . (*Seeing Stafford*) Oh, talking to the Press, are you?

DORCAS No, just passing the time of the day.

153

LEN Enjoying the race, Squire?

STAFFORD Rather.

DORCAS Uncle Len, this is Mr . . .

STAFFORD Mr S. Grimshaw. Hallo.

LEN (*briefly shaking his hand*) How do you do. Len Coker. (*Heading for the slope*) Excuse me, I just have to . . . (*Stopping*) It's odd that. We've got a namesake of yours running in this race. Another Grimshaw. Coincidence.

STAFFORD Ah well. It's a common enough name.

LEN (*dubiously*) Yes, yes. You've covered this race before, haven't you?

STAFFORD Ha ha.

LEN Thought so. Never forget a face. Excuse me. (*Shouting*) Mel! Mel!

MELVYN (*off, distant*) Hallo.

LEN Mel!

Melvyn arrives to join Len at the top of the slope

MELVYN Yes?

LEN We can't see anyone on Durkin's Ridge at all. Can you see anyone?

MELVYN No.

LEN Bloody odd. I mean, the field's often spread out but not as thin as this. I mean, it's been, what, three or four minutes since those two came through. They'll lap 'em all in a minute at this rate. (*To Stafford*) Excuse me. (*To Melvyn*) Keep your eyes peeled.

Melvyn goes off

Len comes down the bank

I think there may be some records broken today, Mr Grimshaw.

STAFFORD (*nodding, hawk-eyed*) Uh-huh, uh-huh.

LEN If you'd care to join us afterwards, we'll be having an informal cup of tea in the Range-Rover.

STAFFORD Possibly will, possibly will.

Melvyn appears at the top of the slope again

MELVYN (*calling*) Uncle Len.

LEN Yes. What is it, son? (*To Stafford, moving away*) Excuse me.

MELVYN I can see one more.

LEN Only one?

MELVYN Yes, he's running very slowly.

LEN This is very peculiar. I mean, there's supposed to be eighteen runners out there somewhere. They can't have disappeared. Let's have a look.

DORCAS Anything I can do?

LEN (*running up the slope and grabbing Melvyn's binoculars*) No. No. (*Looking through the glasses*) That's George Lidgett. That's Major Lidgett, that is. He shouldn't be running in third place.

MELVYN There's something wrong, isn't there?

LEN Sssh. Keep your voice down. The Press are just there. They'd have a field day over this.

MELVYN It's all right. He won't say anything, he's . . .

LEN Sssh. Keep your voice down and get back to your post.

Melvyn goes

Len runs down the hill

(*To Stafford*) Excuse me.

DORCAS Shall I stay here?

LEN Yes, don't move whatever you do. You're always welcome to stroll this way, Mr Grimshaw, if you'd like a better view.

Len goes off to the starting area

DORCAS (*laughing*) Mr Grimshaw! (*Becoming serious*) Nevertheless, Stafford, let us be quite clear . . .

STAFFORD Uh?

DORCAS I have one Mr Grimshaw. He is quite sufficient. I do not want two.

STAFFORD Then get rid of him.

DORCAS No.

STAFFORD I was here first.

MELVYN (*off*) Hooray!

Major Lidgett appears at the top of the hill. He is wiry but seems quite frail, and runs very slowly and carefully. Nevertheless, he is running. He wears a running cap, shorts, and running vest with number 23

DORCAS (*seeing him*) Good lord. (*Gently, to Major Lidgett*) Left round the red flags, right round the blue flags. Thank you.

Len enters from the starting area. He sees Lidgett

LEN Ah, Major Lidgett. (*He falls into step beside him in order to talk to him*) Major Lidgett, where are the others?

Lidgett, with a wave of his hand, disclaims any knowledge

Yes, but where are the rest of the field? They can't have vanished . . .

Lidgett runs off, with Len in pursuit still talking. Melvyn appears at the top of the hill again

MELVYN Did you see that?

DORCAS Yes.

MELVYN He nearly fell down this hole here. It's very dangerous.

DORCAS Well, move the flag.

MELVYN Do you think I should?

DORCAS If it's dangerous, someone will get hurt, won't they?

MELVYN Yes, but . . .

DORCAS Move the flag.

MELVYN O.K.

Melvyn goes off over the slope. Len simultaneously returns with furrowed brow

156

LEN   Dorcas, could you spare me one moment, please?

DORCAS   (*moving to him*) Yes?

LEN   (*to Stafford*) Excuse me.

STAFFORD   Yes.

LEN   (*to Dorcas, in an undertone*) It would appear that we have lost the rest of the field.

DORCAS   (*exclaiming*) Lost it?

LEN   Please – don't raise your voice. Our friend from the Press there will have it in headlines two foot high. And he'd love it, the bastard, he'd love it. It appears that vandals have removed one of our flags.

DORCAS   Oh no.

LEN   Causing the majority of the competitors to go straight on up the B four-eight-one, failing to turn off at the footbridge over Pendon Trickle. Thus they have joined the A four-one-five-five with the result they are, to the best of my knowledge, halfway to Reading.

DORCAS   Oh dear.

LEN   I've sent the loudspeaker van to hail them back, but quite evidently the race is null and void.

DORCAS   Oh dear. Major Lidgett got through.

LEN   I should bloody well hope so. He's been running it for thirty-eight years.

DORCAS   Why didn't the rest of them follow him?

LEN   How could they follow him? He was half a mile behind them.

DORCAS   Are we stopping, then?

LEN   Well, normally that would be the procedure but young Murphy at present is running an extremely promising time. In the circumstances, we feel he should be allowed to run on if he so wishes. I shall be acquainting the remaining runners of the position as they complete the second lap. I'd be grateful meanwhile if you could keep this Press man occupied and as far from the fact as possible.

DORCAS   How?

LEN   Distract him, girl, distract him.

DORCAS O.K.

Melvyn appears again

MELVYN Here they come.
LEN Right, right. (*He runs up the hill*)
MELVYN Simon's in the lead.

Melvyn goes

LEN (*going off over the hill*) Simon is?

Len goes

DORCAS (*rather automatically*) Hooray, hooray.
STAFFORD Anything wrong?
DORCAS No. Just stewards' talk
STAFFORD Ah. There don't seem to be a lot of runners in this race. Is that normal?
DORCAS Oh yes, quite normal.
STAFFORD Ah.

Simon and Len appear side by side at the top of the slope

DORCAS (*to Stafford*) Look out.

Stafford moves away. Simon runs down the hill, looking decidedly more tired, but he remains grim and determined. Len runs beside him, talking softly

LEN ... so the position is that the rest of the field are now on the A four-one-five-five so the question is, do you wish to continue the race or stop at the end of this lap? The decision is entirely in your hands ...

Len and Simon run off, still talking

DORCAS (*over the above*) Left round the red flag, right round the blue flag. Thank you.
STAFFORD Listen, Dorc, I don't think you've quite got my argument. I'm back, that's the point I'm making. I'm back.
DORCAS Stafford, please, I'm ...

Len runs in past her and up the hill

LEN (*as he passes*) He wants to carry on. (*Waving the watch*) Seventeen minutes, twenty-two seconds. It's a good one.

DORCAS Good.

Len runs off over the hill

STAFFORD What I'm saying is let's pick it up again now. I mean, as far as I'm concerned nothing's happened. It can all be the same as it was.

DORCAS But, Staff, a hell of a lot has happened . . . (*She breaks off*)

Murphy appears on the slope, again shadowed by Len, in similar fashion as before

LEN . . . so the position is that the rest of the field are now on the A four-one-five-five, so the question is do you wish to continue the race or stop at the end of this lap? The decision is entirely in your hands . . .

Len and Murphy exit together, still talking

DORCAS (*under the above*) Left round the red flag, right round the blue flag. Thank you.

STAFFORD What are you saying's happened?

DORCAS Well, perhaps nothing has to you. I don't know. Apart from criminally impersonating someone to obtain employment by false pretences. But for me, quite a lot has happened.

STAFFORD What, what?

Len enters. He holds the stopwatch

LEN (*to himself*) Seventeen minutes, forty-eight seconds. (*To Stafford*) Excuse me.

DORCAS (*moving to Len*) Yes.

LEN (*sotto voce*) Murphy would prefer to stop.

DORCAS Oh. You're not going to let him, are you?

LEN   No. The record is still vulnerable. I told him to pull his finger out and get moving. (*Patting her on the arm, and nodding at Stafford*) Good girl, keep him busy.

Len moves off to the starting area again

STAFFORD   The question is, Dorc, what else do you want me to do? What do you want from me? There is a major demonstration of workers solidarity going on in Slough at this very minute. I should be there. Don't you see, I have given up my politics, I have given up my poetry, I hope you've noticed I've even given up smoking. Look, I've shaved, for God's sake. I promise I will never write on your bedroom ceiling again. I won't wake you up in the night to say I love you. I won't ring in on your phone-in programmes to read you love poems.

DORCAS   Shut up, Stafford.

STAFFORD   I won't be there, I promise, when you come home at night with your cocoa.

DORCAS   I said, shut up. I know what you're doing, so shut up.

STAFFORD   Look, Dorc, look. Look at me. I'm really boring and ordinary now, you know. I mean, you stand me next to the real Grimshaw, you'll never know the difference, I promise. I'll do exercises and grow unnecessary muscles, if that's what you'd like.

DORCAS   Stafford . . .

STAFFORD   Yes?

DORCAS   I'm going to hit you with a pole in a minute.

STAFFORD   Go on, go on. Yes, yes, yes.

DORCAS   Why the hell do I always get landed with the lame ducks?

STAFFORD   You know what they say?

DORCAS   What?

STAFFORD   If you don't like lame ducks, you really must stop stamping on their toes.

Melvyn appears at the top of the hill

MELVYN   Here comes Major Lidgett again.

Len runs on from the starting area

LEN   Is that Major Lidgett?

MELVYN   Yes, he's on his way.

Melvyn runs off

DORCAS   Hooray, hooray. He's jolly good for his age, isn't he?

LEN   Yes, he should do this lap in . . .

A distant feeble cry is heard

What's that?

Melvyn appears

MELVYN   Major Lidgett's fallen down a hole.

LEN   (*running up the hill*) Oh, my God.

Len goes off

DORCAS   (*to Melvyn*) Oh dear, didn't you move the flag?

MELVYN   Yes, he fell down the hole on the other side.

STAFFORD   (*at his notebook*) How do you spell Lidgett?

Len returns wearily

DORCAS   How is he?

LEN   He's all right, he's all right. No thanks to someone.

DORCAS   Why?

LEN   Some vandal moved that flag as well, you know. Two yards to the right. He saw the blue flag. Went round the right-hand side, quite correctly and finished up in a seven-foot hole. Now, that's not accidental. It's an inside job by someone with prior knowledge. It's political, I'm convinced of that. They'll do anything for publicity. (*To Stafford*) Don't you dare print this.

DORCAS   Is he all right, Major Lidgett?

LEN   Fortunately, yes. He's not substantially damaged. But it's taken the edge off his enthusiasm, you know. He's given

161

up the race. Brenda's walking him home. (*As he goes*) Tragic, isn't it? First time in thirty-eight years. Tragic.

Len goes out

DORCAS What are you writing?

STAFFORD How do you spell Last Will and Testament?

DORCAS You're being very unfair to me, Stafford. I thought I'd got my life sorted at last. I'd found Simon. For the first time in my life, I'd actually got something Abigail wanted and couldn't have. I mean, that's incidental, I think, but it wasn't a bad feeling after so many years. Suddenly I was O.K. I had a man who was looking after me instead of me looking after him.

STAFFORD But if that's . . .?

DORCAS That's what it was, Stafford. Always. Me looking after you. Me making decisions. Me telling you what to do next, where to go.

STAFFORD Because that's what you wanted to do.

DORCAS My God, did you think that?

STAFFORD Well, tell me this. How do you like it the other way round, eh? How do you like being told by him?

DORCAS He doesn't.

STAFFORD He will.

DORCAS He won't.

STAFFORD He'll keep at you till he does. He won't stop till he's running everything. I've seen that type before. They're office managers, all of them. He'll get his way. Even if he has to do it by force.

DORCAS Well, perhaps that's what I do want then.

STAFFORD You don't want that. If you'd've wanted that, you'd've married your brother-in-law, wouldn't you? Patrick?

DORCAS All right, what do I want then? You say.

STAFFORD Me.

DORCAS No, Staff, I'm sorry. There's got to be more to life than nurse-maiding you.

STAFFORD   Ah-ha, but will you ever find it?

DORCAS   What can you offer me?

STAFFORD   Think.

DORCAS   That nobody else can.

STAFFORD   Think.

DORCAS   That Simon can't.

STAFFORD   Think hard.

DORCAS   What is there about you that is so marvellous?

STAFFORD   Think, think.

DORCAS   No good.

STAFFORD   Think, remember.

DORCAS   I can't.

STAFFORD   (*moving very close to Dorcas*) Rack your brains. Rack your loins. It is I, Stafford T. Wilkins alias S. Grimshaw, ace reporter . . .

Len comes on hurriedly and goes straight up the hill, hardly noticing them

LEN   (*stopwatch in hand*) Your lad's doing well. He's heading for the record.

Melvyn comes on over the hill

MELVYN   He's coming.

LEN   Come on, Grimshaw!

MELVYN   Grimshaw!

STAFFORD   (*to Dorcas*) Hear that, they're shouting for me.

LEN   Come on, Grimshaw!

MELVYN   Come on, Grimshaw!

Other voices are heard at the finishing line shouting for Grimshaw

STAFFORD   Come on, Grimshaw!

DORCAS   (*lying back against the bank*) Come on, Grimshaw!

STAFFORD   That's it. Let's hear it again.

DORCAS   Come on, come on, come on.

MELVYN   Come on, Grimshaw.

LEN   Here he comes.

STAFFORD   Here comes Grimshaw.
DORCAS   Here comes Grimshaw.

Stafford lies with Dorcas

MELVYN   Bravo!

Simon runs on, a look of triumph in his eyes: a man with a record in sight. He reaches the bottom of the bank. As he does so, Stafford and Dorcas, locked together, roll into his path

LEN   Keep going, keep going. You've got it.

Simon stops, breathing heavily. He stares at Dorcas and Stafford

DORCAS   (*sitting up*) Oh. God. Look, Grimshaw – I mean, Simon . . .

Simon stares, shaking his head trying to get his breath

LEN   Go on, man, go on. You can't stop. You've got ten seconds: nine seconds to beat that record.
STAFFORD   (*to Simon*) You want to hit me? Hit me.
LEN   Eight.
STAFFORD   I've chosen for her, you see.
LEN   Seven.
STAFFORD   You don't need her.
LEN   Six.
STAFFORD   She needs me.
LEN   Five.
STAFFORD   It's no use asking her to choose.
LEN   Four.
STAFFORD   She only chooses wrong.
LEN   Three.
STAFFORD   Always.
LEN   Two.
STAFFORD   Go on.
LEN   One.
STAFFORD   Win your race. Leave her alone.
LEN   (*banging his stopwatch in irritation*) Oh God. Well, that's

it, isn't it? All over, there goes the record. What's the matter with the lad?

Murphy appears at the top of the hill. He is completely clapped out. He stands clasping his side in great pain from a stitch. He surveys the scene

MELVYN (*seeing Murphy*) Look out, Simon.

Murphy sees Simon

LEN Come on, Murphy. You can still win, boy.

DORCAS (*gently*) Go on, Simon. Left round red flag, right round the blue one.

Simon looks at Dorcas and Stafford, then at Murphy. Murphy starts to come down the slope

LEN Run, Murphy. Run, lad.

DORCAS Run, Simon.

MELVYN Go on, Simon, run.

Simon exits round the flags followed by Murphy. Melvyn follows

MELVYN (*returning from the finishing line, briefly*) He's won. Simon's won. He's won.

DORCAS Hooray, hooray.

Melvyn goes off

LEN (*following, and looking at his stopwatch in disgust: to Stafford*) And I rather expect the Press to conduct themselves better than that, you know. That's an accredited steward.

Len goes off to the finishing line. As he goes, the sound of cheers

DORCAS Well? You want to come home to tea?

STAFFORD O.K.

DORCAS What about your story? Do you have to file it, or whatever you call it?

STAFFORD No, no. It'll keep, it'll keep. We'll probably put it on the spike, you know. Run it as a colour feature later.

165

DORCAS (*in realization*) You aren't working for any newspaper at all, are you?

STAFFORD No.

DORCAS You haven't given up writing poetry?

STAFFORD No.

DORCAS Or your politics?

STAFFORD No.

DORCAS Or smoking?

STAFFORD I'm trying.

DORCAS You've still got no money.

STAFFORD No.

DORCAS You little – maggot. Where did you get those clothes, then, if you've got no money?

STAFFORD I found them on the bench over there. (*Indicating the starting area*) I think they belong to that old git. Major Lidgett.

DORCAS (*closing her eyes in exasperation*) All right, that's it. That is finally it. You have just thrown away your very last . . . Aaark!

Stafford has lifted her off her feet. He swings her over his shoulder cave-man fashion and lopes up the hill with her

Stafford! Stafford, put me down, Stafford. Where are we going . . .

STAFFORD (*with a leer*) We're going for a run . . .

DORCAS (*resignedly*) Oh, Stafford.

They disappear over the hill

The Lights fade

Act Two

Scene 2 Footnote

The same. A Saturday afternoon in November, about 3 p.m. It is a cold but dry day, slightly frosty

As the scene starts, immediately Ralph comes hurrying on. He is dressed very smartly in his best suit and a colourful tie. He has his hat on but no coat. The effect is ruined somewhat by his footwear. A pair of cheerful, worn bedroom slippers. In his buttonhole, a carnation. He is followed by Len, also in his best suit, probably the same as at the start though his tie, too, is brighter, reflecting a more cheerful occasion. He, also, wears a carnation. On his arm is Rita dressed in her wedding outfit with floral spray doing her best to add cheer to the proceedings, through her usual tide of troubles

RALPH   ... Now I know none of you are going to love me for this but I think you're going to thank me for it when you've seen this view. Now, this here ... Len, Rita ... this spot here ... the day I got married to Amy, we came to this very spot and we rushed up that hill, Amy still in her long wedding dress ... yes. (*He muses*)

RITA   It must have got very muddy.

RALPH   I remember we stood there for so long watching the sun going down, back there the whole reception sitting there waiting for us. They couldn't start, you see.

RITA   Must have caused a bit of a stir.

LEN   It did.

RALPH   Oh well – we were all mad in those days.

LEN   Yes.

RITA   Yes, yes. Don't spoil your bedroom slippers, will you, Ralph?

RALPH   No, no.

LEN   Find them more comfortable to wear these days, do you?

RALPH   Not really.

167

LEN Ah.

RITA Yes, yes.

RALPH Where are the rest of them? (*Shouting back*) Come on, you lot. I'm waiting to show you this view.

Melvyn enters with Brenda. Brenda is in full conventional wedding dress, Melvyn in his suit and carnation

MELVYN Sorry.

LEN Ah, the happy couple.

RITA (*without a lot of fire*) Hooray, hooray.

Melvyn kisses Brenda

RALPH Don't keep doing that, boy. You'll give her some dreadful disease. Now, we're all going up the slope.

MELVYN Here we go again.

RALPH (*greatly amused by this*) Here we go again, he says. Here we go again. (*Seizing Rita's arm*) Come on, Rita, we'll get you up there.

RITA Oh, I don't know if I can . . .

RALPH Come on, come on.

LEN Careful with her now, Ralph, the ground's a bit hard.

RALPH (*to Rita*) We'll get you over the difficult bits, don't you worry.

MELVYN Why don't you put your shoes on, Dad? Have you lost them again?

RALPH Lost them, he says. 'Course I haven't lost them, you daft dimple. Now I've told you before, I've told you this – listen to your feet. Listen to your feet. And you know why? Because where are your feet?

MELVYN (*repeating as if by heart*) On the other end of my body to my head.

RALPH Correct. On their own. Right down there.

Len anxiously watches Rita as Ralph gesticulates with her

LEN You'll be careful with her, won't you, Ralph?

RALPH Yes, yes. You see, your feet are your distant branch

office. They're your outposts. If you're going to get trouble, it generally starts miles from your H.Q. (*He taps his head*) If you neglect your feet, they get a chip on their shoulder. Talk to your feet and you'll live to be ninety-nine. Chat to your tootsies. I've told all my patients that. Bit by bit, none of them needed to come back. Never saw them again. All cured.

LEN That's a very interesting theory.

RALPH (*heaving Rita up the remaining slope*) All right, Rita. (*Over his shoulder*) And don't make them wear shoes if they don't want to. They never asked to, did they?

LEN (*to Melvyn, nervously, as he watches*) As long as he doesn't push her down that hole again. The last time it didn't do her a scrap of good, you know.

Ralph and Rita stop for a breather

(*To Melvyn and Brenda*) I hear you two are going to open a shop.

MELVYN That's right.

LEN Where did you find the money for that then?

MELVYN We borrowed it.

LEN Dear, dear, dear. Into debt before you've begun. What sort of start is that, eh?

MELVYN It'll be O.K.

LEN It'll be O.K. till you have to pay it back. (*Wagging a finger at Brenda*) Money has to be paid back, you know.

BRENDA Well, in our case, I think the risks are fairly minimal. I've negotiated the interest privately at a fixed eight per cent and it's compounded at monthly stops with the repayment of the initial capital and the corresponding payment of interest only becoming due at the start of each new financial year.

LEN (*digesting this*) Oh well then, you'll probably be just about all right then.

RALPH Come on, you lot. Rita and I have scaled the mountain.

169

MELVYN Hang on.

Melvyn sweeps Brenda up in his arms

LEN What sort of shop are you opening then?

MELVYN A toyshop. (*He runs up the slope carrying Brenda*)

LEN (*muttering*) I don't know why I bothered to ask. (*He starts to follow*)

RALPH (*meanwhile watching Melvyn's antics*) Bravo, bravo.

> *Dorcas appears dressed attractively for the wedding. Following her a little way behind is Stafford who has been given a new outfit for the occasion but manages to make it look already quite old*

DORCAS (*calling*) Pa, we're paying for these cars by the hour, you know.

Melvyn and Brenda go off over the hill

RALPH Come up here, Abi. It's glorious, glorious.

DORCAS Dorcas, Father.

RALPH That's right, bring Dorcas as well. We want all of you up here. And the best man. Where's the best man? Where's that young Simon?

Ralph goes out over the hill, following Melvyn and Brenda

RITA (*who has been abandoned suddenly*) He's not right, you know, is he?

DORCAS He certainly isn't.

LEN He's got this thing about feet. He keeps grabbing folk by the feet all the time.

RITA I mean, when he does it suddenly he up-ends you, you know.

LEN He up-ended Rita.

DORCAS Oh dear.

RITA He did. I went right over, didn't I?

LEN Right. Over she went. Chest over cheeks.

RITA Chest over cheeks.

Len and Rita disappear over the hill

Dorcas stands impatiently, unsure how to recall the party. Stafford stands ruminatively

DORCAS (*absently*) Stafford, tuck your shirt in, love. Well, I hope they hurry up. (*To Stafford again*) Now that wasn't too bad, was it? I mean, you stood in the church and you weren't struck by lightning. O.K.?

STAFFORD Yeah.

DORCAS You'll get something to eat in a minute. That'll cheer you up.

STAFFORD Great. Yeah . . .

Abigail comes on hurriedly, also dressed well and expensively

ABIGAIL What the hell is Pa playing at? Brenda's mother is droning on in that car there, she's driving Patrick mad. I can see he's beginning to foam.

DORCAS She's driving us all nuts. What are you talking about?

ABIGAIL (*calling up the slope*) Pa! (*Slight pause*) Father, dear!

DORCAS It's no use.

ABIGAIL Well, we're going to have to drive off and leave him in a minute. The whole wedding's a fiasco anyway. That large pregnant thing lumping up the aisle.

DORCAS It doesn't show.

ABIGAIL Well, I'll give them a year. I mean, opening a toyshop. Honestly. Who needs a toyshop in this place?

DORCAS People who have children. You will soon.

ABIGAIL (*laughing drily*) We'll see. I think Patrick plans to wean our child straight on to calculators.

Stafford wanders away, head down, punching with one arm

DORCAS Don't wander too far off, will you, Staff?

STAFFORD No.

Stafford goes off

DORCAS (*semi-apologetically*) He's writing a poem. At least I think he is.

171

ABIGAIL He's looking a bit better, isn't he? Has he been washing more?

DORCAS No, no, no. That's next year's job.

ABIGAIL Look, if Father really does drive you potty and you can't stand looking after him another minute, then he'll have to come and live with us. But now with the baby coming, I really don't think . . .

DORCAS No, no, that's O.K. He's fine. Except he thinks I'm you half the time.

ABIGAIL How extraordinary. We're hardly alike. And you really won't miss your job?

DORCAS No. And it means Stafford's got to work which is good. It'll give him an incentive.

Patrick arrives, similarly dressed to the others

PATRICK (*to Abigail*) Darling, could you possibly whistle your father and put him back on his lead, please. I am stuck in the back of a car with a woman who has the political views of Attila the Hun and I'm about to let her have it between her hat.

ABIGAIL Please be polite to the bride's mother.

PATRICK The bride is shortly to be orphaned. Hurry up. (*He turns to go*)

Simon hurries on, nearly colliding with Patrick

SIMON Sorry. Beg your pardon. After you.

PATRICK No, after you. You're the best man, after all.

SIMON Yes, true . . .

PATRICK Well, for today anyway.

Patrick goes

Simon laughs

SIMON (*to the women*) Is the old boy coming then?

ABIGAIL I've no idea.

SIMON Only the drivers are getting a bit stroppy. I slipped them both a quid. All the same . . . I'll give him a yell, shall I? (*No reply*) Yes. Sorry. I'm afraid Mother's going on a bit. Proud Mama, you know. Yes. Right.

Simon runs up the slope. He stops briefly, aware that both women are staring at him. He turns, smiles at them both and winks rather self-consciously. He goes off over the hill

ABIGAIL (*when Simon has gone*) I have to say it, he's a very silly man, isn't he? I mean, when I first met him, I don't think I realized quite how silly he was. I suppose I was taken in by all the sunburn and teeth and things. Well, weren't we all?

DORCAS Yes, I know what you mean.

ABIGAIL I don't know about you but I'm absolutely certain I made the right decision there. I expect you feel the same.

DORCAS Yes. (*With less conviction*) Oh yes – I think so.

ABIGAIL Aren't you sure?

DORCAS No. What I mean is, I think I made a decision.

ABIGAIL Well, you decided, didn't you? You decided, what-ever the temptations, to stay with thingy – Stafford. And I decided, God help me, to stick with Patrick.

DORCAS (*not really convinced*) Yes, I expect we did. Anyhow, the important thing is for us to *feel* we've made decisions, isn't it? Otherwise, everything would just be so pointless . . .

ABIGAIL Yes, quite right. Now, next decision. Which of us is to travel home the rest of the way in the car which contains the bride's mother and her hat?

DORCAS (*smiling*) Tell you what. I'll toss you for it.

They start to go

ABIGAIL God, she's a dreary woman. I was talking to her in the car just now. Everything I said – gneer, gneer, gneer.

DORCAS Gneer, gneer, gneer.

ABIGAIL I mean, Mel's not getting stuck with that, is he?

Dorcas and Abigail go

The Lights fade to a BLACKOUT

Notes

The notes in this edition are intended to serve the needs of overseas students as well as those of British-born users.

Inverted commas indicate references to stage directions.

An asterisk (*) indicates a colloquialism or a specific idiom.

List of characters

Abigail: a name used traditionally for a lady's maid. The name first appeared in the Bible (Samuel 1: 25) when it referred to one of King David's wives.

Dorcas: another biblical name (Acts 9); a woman who made coats and other garments for widows.

Len: short for Leonard.

Act One Scene One Prologue

1 *'Pendon Common'*: Pendon is the fictitious name of a small town to the west of London, well within daily commuting distance to and from London. A common is a piece of land for the use of the whole community including, traditionally, free grazing for cattle, horses and other animals.

'plinth': a block supporting the bench.

'incongruously': out of place, the dark figures look odd against the meadow.

'deadpan': expressionless.

2 *vandals*: people who destroy for the sake of destroying.

wallop: a good thrashing.

4 *fifty-guinea*: a guinea (no longer in use) was worth one pound and five pence. Fifty guineas would be fifty-two pounds and fifty pence.

174

5 *rabbiting**: chattering.

6 *linseed oil*: oil used to preserve and give a polished finish to raw wood.

7 *gallivant*: spend time engaged in frivolous activities.

   what-have-yous*: whatever you like to call the relationships.

8 '*in tow*': Brenda is being pulled along by Melvyn.

10 *injury time*: extra time allowed by a referee during a match to make up for time lost as a result of an injury.

11 *Gneeer**: Abigail is imitating the nasal way in which Brenda speaks.

12 *fascist*: originally a member of a political party in Italy; now used to refer to anyone with extreme right wing, nationalist views.

12 *an oil man*: someone who works for an oil company.

13 *Christmas dances at the rugger club*: grand local events when women would be invited socially to join men in their rugby club.

Act One Scene Two Abigail

18 '*paraphernalia*': accessories, often unnecessary. Here it would be a bag of mixed objects used for the picnic.

19 *Oh, cobblers**: don't talk rubbish.

   a Knightsbridge socialite: a rich person living in Knightsbridge, a fashionable district in south-west London.

   B.B.C.: British Broadcasting Corporation.

   I blew it*: I made a mess of my interview.

24 *agenda*: programme of business to be dealt with at a meeting.

   minutes: summary of proceedings at a meeting.

27 '*Colour Supplement*': many British newspapers have a weekly colour magazine, usually on Sundays.

29 *P.E.*: Physical Education.

30 *misanthropic*: distrusting and disliking all fellow human beings.

the sonnets: reference to Shakespeare's Sonnet III. The sonnets are much concerned with love and the passing of time.

33 *Merc*: short for Mercedes, a luxurious German motor car.

34 *Spartan*: the inhabitants of ancient Sparta in Greece were known for their courage, plain living and harsh discipline. Patrick here means that cycling as opposed to motoring is an unnecessarily rigorous way of going about the countryside.

35 '*sotto voce*': speaking in an undertone.

38 *hoof*: horse's foot.

40 '*half rounds*': two slices of bread with a filling between them make a round; when cut in half, they make a half round.

43 *cross-country derby*: Derby refers to the famous horse race run on Epsom Downs (Surrey) in early June. A cross-country race is run by people across open country. This particular event is a hard-run, keenly-fought competition of local importance.

45 *old lumpkin**: Tony Lumpkin was a loutish, good-natured character in the eighteenth-century comedy *She Stoops to Conquer* by Oliver Goldsmith. Ralph here means it as a term of endearment.

49 *It's to do with more than that* . . .: Stafford plucks up courage to repeat some left-wing political jargon which he has obviously picked up from somewhere. He attacks the B.B.C. for being in the hands of a middle-class management whose aims are (according to Stafford) to present programmes of low quality to a mass audience and to ignore the truly creative artist.
morons: idiots.

50 *St Vitus's Dance*: the popular name for chorea, a nervous disease causing irregular and involuntary movements of the face or limbs.

Act One Scene Two Dorcas

54 *'Ben Gunn-like'*: Ben Gunn is the pirate character in Robert
Louis Stevenson's novel *Treasure Island* who stared with a
haunted look when he first saw humans on the island.
metabolisms: changes in the chemical make-up of the
human body.

56 *cocked up**: damaged.

64 *quid**: pounds.

66 *Byron and Shelley*: poets of the Romantic period, early nine-
teenth century.

68 *a depraved mind*: a dirty mind.

70 *gobbit**: unflattering remark about Stafford's small size.

73 *Strathclyde*: a western region of Scotland centred on
Glasgow. By confusing Stafford's name (Stafford is the
county town of Staffordshire in England) Ralph indicates
the low opinion he has of his daughter's boy friend.

88 *Geronimo*: an Indian war cry. Geronimo was the name
taken by a chieftain who led an Indian campaign against
the whites in 1885.

89 *craven*: cowardly.

Act Two Scene One Abigail

90 *'falsetto'*: a forced voice of a register above the natural.

91 *'sarcasm'*: mocking scorn.
Mafeking: a town in South Africa where the British were
besieged by the Boers for seven months in 1899/1900. The
long duration of the siege led people in Britain to consider
it a major disaster.
*Yep**: slang for yes.

94 *Town Hall level*: the Town Hall is the centre of local
government. Patrick is sarcastic about Len's obedience to
what he considers a rather low-level authority.

95 *coven*: a gang of witches.

palaver*: idle talk.

Slough: an industrial town between Reading and London, therefore not far from Pendon.

96 '*anorak*': a half-length coat made of waterproof material.

97 *whippet*: a racing dog, cross between a greyhound and a terrier.

102 *frolic*: amusement.

103 *tryst*: arranged secret meeting.

104 *delicatessen*: a shop selling specially prepared foods.

Amy Johnson: the first woman aviator to fly solo from England to Australia when she made a record flight to India in six days. She lived from 1904 to 1941 (killed during the war).

105 *coquilles St Jacques*: a tasty French fish recipe for scallops served in their shells.

brown windsor soup: a plain but wholesome soup, like gravy.

105 *K41*: Mozart's Symphony No. 41.

108 *status quo*: things as they stand.

109 *claustrophobia*: fear of being in a confined place.

115 *prat**: a word, no longer used, to describe a rogue.

117 *the local rag**: the local newspaper.

Chief Executive: the most senior official in local government.

118 *sixty-two Latour*: one of the most expensive red Bordeaux wines, held in high esteem by connoisseurs. This bottle dates from 1962.

123 *Voilà*: French for 'there'.

126 *pole-axed*: literally means slaughtered with an axe. Len once again uses words without knowing their real meaning.

127 *yurck*: sound made by Patrick as he is being yanked into the tent.

Act Two Scene One Dorcas

130 *peaceful demonstration in Slough*: Len is sarcastic. He refers to a march to demonstrate for peace.

133 *Blimey O'Reilly**: slang for 'Good Heavens!' Blimey is cockney (London) slang for 'Blind me!'

134 *punnet**: literally, a small, shallow basket. Len is being derogatory about Melvyn.

137 *lap*: overtake.

141 *squirt**: dwarf.

142 *Michelangelo*: great Italian artist of the fifteenth century who painted the ceiling of the Sistine Chapel in the Vatican in Rome.

erk*: the lowest of the low; originally used to describe an ordinary naval or air force rating.

144 *egocentric*: someone who sees himself as the centre of the universe, who has an exaggerated opinion of himself.

145 *gimlet-like*: watchful.

felon: criminal.

147 *Arts Council*: an institution set up by the Government to allocate financial grants to the arts.

148 *squire*: in the past, a formal title for a gentleman with property in the country. Len uses it in an ingratiating way, to show he is on friendly terms with the 'press reporter', but he doesn't know his name.

berk*: slang for idiot.

150 *Pools*: football pool lottery.

151 *Lord Northcliffe*: famous newspaper proprietor who died in 1922.

Manchester United: one of the best known First Division football teams.

153 *nom de plume*: French for pen name, a name adopted by a writer instead of his or her real name.

154 *peeled**: wide open.

165 *'clapped out'**: exhausted.

Act Two Scene Two Footnote

169 *H.Q.*: Headquarters.

Well, in our case . . .: Brenda takes everyone by surprise by suddenly displaying expert knowledge of finance.

171 '*ruminatively*': deep in thought.

172 *potty**: out of your mind.

Attila the Hun: a barbaric king who conquered and laid waste to Western Europe in the fifth century.

stroppy*: angry; being difficult.

173 *I slipped them both a quid**: I gave them both a pound as a tip.

Suggested further reading

Michael Billington, *Alan Ayckbourn*, Macmillan Modern Dramatists, 1983.

John Elsom, *Post-war British Theatre*, Routledge and Kegan Paul, 1976.

Stephen Joseph, *Theatre in the Round*, Barrie and Rockliff, 1967.

Oleg Kerensky, *The New British Drama*, Hamish Hamilton, 1977.

Benedict Nightingale, *An Introduction to 50 Modern British Plays*, Pan Books, 1982.

John Russell Taylor, *The Second Wave*, Methuen, 1971.

Ian Watson, *Conversations with Ayckbourn*, Macdonald, 1981.

Study assignments

This chapter is in three parts: (i) study tasks for discussion and writing on separate scenes; (ii) writing tasks for the whole play; and (iii) oral work on the whole play.

Studying the play scene by scene

Act One Scene One Prologue

1 In his introduction to the play the author, Alan Ayckbourn, writes: 'Characters should not only discuss what they've done or what they're about to do but should also be *seen* to do it.'

Make a list of all the moments in this first scene where characters are seen in action. Begin with the very first sight of the characters, all dressed in black or dark clothes, standing in various positions on a steep, grassy slope.

Who are they? What are their relationships to one another? What is so incongruous (this word will have been explained in the notes) about this sight?

2 By the end of this scene what have you discovered about every one of the ten characters? Which character or characters do you feel you already know better than the others? Why? How would you recognise them if you saw them in the street?

3 What are the various disasters that happen in this scene? To whom do they happen?

4 Abigail asks her sister Dorcas who is a broadcaster for the local radio station: 'Do people listen?' Why do you think she asks this question? Why does Dorcas 'flare' in her reply? What else do the sisters squabble about? Do they agree about anything?

5 Which is the most important moment in this scene?

6 At the end of the scene an actress has to make a choice either 'prearranged but preferably random'. Choose three people to play Abigail, Dorcas and Simon. Act out, using your own words, the tossing of the coin and a reaction by one character who has to make a quick decision. Act this brief scene twice: the first time with a decision made spontaneously by one character, the second time with a prearranged decision.

What is the difference? What would you have to do to make the audience believe that both decisions were spontaneous?

Act One Scene Two Abigail

1 Think again of the importance of characters seen in action. Make a list of all the moments in this scene when the ten main characters come into conflict with external events like the wasps or the rain shower.

2 The scene ends in chaos. Discuss how every character contributes to this chaos.

3 You may have had similar experiences at a family picnic. With whom do you sympathize in this scene? Why?

4 The scene follows Abigail's decision to leave with Simon. Yet Dorcas seems to be the more important of the two sisters in this scene. Why should this be so? Melvyn says to her: 'Don't keep on at her, Dorc' (page 20). Find examples where Dorcas 'keeps on' at someone.

5 Dorcas also has a certain way of running herself down to other people, of deliberately belittling herself. When she talks with Simon about Abigail (page 29) she says:

Abi's a person who expects rather a lot from life . . .

183

Let's face it, most of us are just ordinary people. Average. Like you and me.

What does she really want Simon to understand by all this? How does Simon react?

In a play what characters say may be different from what they think or what they would like to say. Look at the following dialogue (page 30):

DORCAS I don't expect anything much from anyone and as a result, I'm frequently quite pleasantly surprised. It probably means I'm lacking in imagination or something.

What is going on in Dorcas's mind at that moment? A few moments later she says, 'I mean, I know I'm not beautiful in the conventional sense.' What does she really mean? What do we learn about Dorcas in this scene?

6 The scene develops further the theme of making choices. Abigail's husband Patrick also has to make a choice. What is his choice? Is he free to make it?

7 Act out in your own words either a scene after the picnic when Abigail and Dorcas are alone and go over the day's events with absolute frankness or a scene when Patrick and Simon happen to meet later that day. Remember about characters seen in some action.

Act One Scene Two Dorcas

1 Remember that most of the audiences seeing this scene will not know the parallel scene – Scene Two Abigail. What are the new developments?

2 Discuss the similarities as well as the differences between this scene and Scene Two Abigail?

3 Abigail is 'restless and discontent' from the start. From your group choose one member to play Abigail. The rest are her

'judges'. Giving evidence from the text accuse her of being restless, discontent, unpleasant to her husband, deliberately undermining her sister, going on needlessly at her brother, of general anti-social behaviour. As Abigail, try to defend yourself against these charges.

4 So far Melvyn and Brenda appear to be very much over-shadowed by the more forceful characters. Improvise a scene in which Melvyn and Brenda are alone together. Where would you place them? What would they talk about? In the play we never hear them make any comments on the other members of the family. Would they do so by themselves? How would you make this scene dramatic?

5 The author writes in the preface that the actors had a nightly dread of getting the complicated mechanics of the sandwich scene wrong. This also had two different versions. The arrangement here was as follows: *Rita* was supposed to have made eight half rounds of egg and tomato sandwiches. She has actually made cheese and tomato, and sardine and cucumber. *Abigail* has made eight half rounds of cheese and tomato sandwiches as well as sardine and cucumber, as planned.

To make sure that everyone gets a fair share of the two sand-wich fillings Dorcas decides to organise the party. Melvyn exchanges two sandwiches with Len, Simon with Rita, Brenda with Abigail, Ralph with Dorcas. Who is left out?

In Act One Scene Two Abigail, *Dorcas* has made four half-rounds of nut sandwiches for Stafford and ham sandwiches for the rest; there are eight plates. *Rita* made egg and tomato, cheese and tomato, and sardine and cucumber sandwiches. In the general confusion the sandwiches get mixed up. Make a list of the characters and against every name write which sandwiches they get.

Using your own words as well as paper plates and some food act out both versions of the sandwich scene. You will need groups of nine and, perhaps, a director. Use simple language as one would at a picnic when handing out food. What happens if someone makes a mistake? How can you quickly cover up such a mistake? Can you understand the actors' dread of getting it wrong in front of an audience?

Act Two Scene One Abigail

1 What are all the unexpected events that happen in this scene?

2 Which is the most important moment to you? Why? Which are the funniest moments?

3 The author writes in the preface: 'Simon is beginning to show his real colours.' What are these 'real colours'?

4 What is there in the character of Patrick that will make Abigail decide to return to him? Does she get what she deserves?

5 For acting out: either in the character of *Abigail*, a sadder but wiser woman, you want to help a friend who is bored with her married life. Tell her of your experience and the decision you made. How much of the would-be romantic night under canvas would you choose to tell her? Or, in the character of *Patrick*, who has also learnt something, you want to help a friend who has told you of his wife's infidelity. Tell him of your experience. Remember that Patrick is a strong man and blessed with a sense of humour.

6 In the character of Murphy, the police constable, make a report to your inspector on that night's events as you witnessed them.

7 Imagine that, as a resident of Pendon, you walked your dog late that night on the Common and you saw all these events. Write a letter to the *Pendon Gazette* expressing your indignation that such things happen in Pendon.

Act Two Scene One Dorcas

1 Compare this scene with the parallel one in Act Two Scene One Abigail. If you had to advise someone who could see the play only once, which version would you tell him or her to go and see: the night under canvas or the cross-country race? Give your reasons for your choice.

2 Len emerges as an important character in this scene. What have you found out about Len so far? What part does he play in Abigail's and Dorcas's infidelities?

3 A new character appears in this scene – Major Lidgett. What do we know about him? How important is he to the action? What would happen if he did not appear?

4 Dorcas and Simon are both irritable for different reasons. What are the reasons? Their irritability flares up into anger and near violence. Why?

5 Just as Patrick became a much stronger man in the parallel scene, so Stafford becomes more interesting in this scene. Dorcas has a choice between Simon and Stafford. Why does she choose Stafford? What can Stafford offer her?

Act Two Scene Two Footnote

1 Are there any surprising developments in the last scene?

2 There is always a risk that the last scene in a comedy comes as an anti-climax. How does the author avoid an anti-climax in this play?

3 Imagine a different ending to the play. Act it out in your own words.

4 Will Abigail and Dorcas stay with their chosen partners? What might these couples be like ten years later? Twenty years later?

5 Look at this dialogue:

> ABIGAIL   Well, you decided, didn't you? You decided, what-
> ever the temptations, to stay with thingy – Stafford. And
> I decided, God help me, to stick with Patrick.
>
> DORCAS (*not really convinced*) Yes, I expect we did. Anyhow,
> the important thing is for us to *feel* we've made decisions,
> isn't it? Otherwise, everything would be just so point-
> less. . .

What does Dorcas mean by this? What would be so 'pointless' otherwise? What is the difference between making a
decision and feeling that you have made one? Does this last
scene tell us anything about the sisters that we didn't know
before?

Considering the whole play

1 Choose one or more of the main characters of the play and
write a short biography about them. Use your knowledge
of the play to imagine their childhood days, schooling,
training, likes and dislikes, adventures, holidays, hopes and
disappointments, achievements and failures.

2 Suppose that Alan Ayckbourn has accepted an invitation
to be interviewed by you and your group. Compile a list
of questions about the play which you would like to ask
him. Then choose any one of these questions, and, as the
author of the play, try to write a detailed answer.

3 You are the stage manager of the company presenting the
play and responsible for a smooth performance. One
particular evening it was decided between you and the
actors that after Act One Scene One Abigail should leave
with Simon. Acting on impulse and without warning
anyone, the actress playing Dorcas sweeps Simon off with
her instead. There is no interval between the two scenes.
Confusion is caused. Write a letter to the management

(invent name and address) presenting the play. Describe clearly what happened, what problems were caused, how you tried to solve them.

4 'Ayckbourn's characters are very ordinary people, but the things that happen to them are not ordinary.' Discuss this statement.

5 What would the play gain and lose from being filmed instead of being played live on stage?

6 Using this play as an example attempt to show why Ayckbourn is such a popular playwright.

7 'What is really remarkable [about Ayckbourn as dramatist] is his constant attempt to find out what you can do on a stage.' Give examples from this play to show some of the surprising things you can do on a stage.

8 'There is a danger that the dazzling technique of the play overshadows the characters and situations.' Do you agree?

9 'In the end Brenda and Melvyn have the last laugh.' In what way have they the last laugh?

10 'We get what we deserve.' Is this true of the characters in the play?

Oral work

1 Suppose that Simon had really turned out to be a hand-some, attractive, intelligent hero instead of a dull nonentity, what difference would this have made to the story?

2 Abigail is torn between husband and lover; Dorcas be-tween two boyfriends. Does this make any difference to the story as a whole?

3 'I've learned that to be very funny you need to be very sad. All good comedy should make you cry, otherwise you're probably examining characters in insufficient

depth' (Ayckbourn). Is there anything that is sad in this play? Do you find anything sad about the characters, or the situations in which they find themselves, or in both?

4 Throughout the six scenes of the play Abigail and Dorcas are shown alone together in brief scenes. Find these and study them carefully. What are the 'sisterly feelings' that exist between them?

5 Now imagine a similar play about 'brotherly feelings'. What differences would there be? How would the characters of Simon, Patrick and Stafford be different in that case?

6 Which characters still hold out hope for development as human beings? Which ones are locked in a world of their own in which no hope for growth is possible?

7 Attempt a rehearsed reading of part of the play – as an example, the beginning of the very first scene. You will need ten characters and a director. Find a space, which need not be very large. With the help of chairs, boxes or tables create different levels to represent Pendon Common. This exercise is based on the assumption that you have about ten to fifteen minutes on at least five occasions.

DAY ONE

Allocate the ten parts and then ask the actors to find a space for themselves. It is unlikely that at first they will be standing in the best positions from a dramatic point of view. You start with two certainties:

(i) Ralph, the newly widowed father, should be the central figure;

(ii) Simon, the only outsider, should stand somewhat apart.

Group the rest in the most interesting way you can devise. Then ask every actor to show, by an expression or an action, one aspect of the character by which they could be recognised. Abigail, for example, could look longingly at Simon. Then freeze the group as if for a photograph. Repeat several times.

DAY TWO

Starting in the same position read through the first page and a half of the text, up to the moment where Ralph – followed by Melvyn and Brenda – has 'vanished momentarily over the top of the hill'. This first readthrough will be rather meaningless. Now discuss how you would begin the play. How long would you stand still at the beginning? What might Ralph have said before the play actually begins? What does his 'yes' mean? Rehearse the opening of the scene. Then discuss among yourselves what every character might be doing during this scene without distracting from Ralph, the central figure. Ralph does not listen to anyone. Simon and Stafford have nothing to say. What might they be doing?

DAY THREE

Once the dialogue begins, the actors would not stand still throughout the scene. Who moves where, when, why? Read through again. This time make sure that

 (i) the actors are in character and seen in some action;
(ii) they move without bumping into one another or masking each other.

DAY FOUR

In today's rehearsal make sure that there are no meaningless gaps in dialogue. Nobody listens to anyone else. There should not be even one second's gap between one actor finishing a line and another one beginning. The conversation overlaps – but without gabbling. Try this several times, and you will begin to understand the difference between pace and speed in the theatre. You may even find that actors will begin to know their lines by heart.

DAY FIVE

Polish this scene as if for a performance and then show it to the other groups.

191